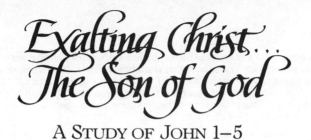

Exalting Christ... The Son of God

A Study of John 1–5

Bible Study Guide

From the Bible-teaching ministry of

Charles R. Swindoll

Insight for Living

Charles R. Swindoll is a graduate of Dallas Theological Seminary and has served in pastorates for more than twenty-four years, including churches in Texas, New England, and California. Since 1971 he has served as senior pastor of the First Evangelical Free Church of Fullerton, California. Chuck's radio program, "Insight for Living," began in 1979. In addition to his church and radio ministries, Chuck has written twenty-three books and numerous booklets on a variety of subjects.

Based on the outlines of Chuck's sermons, the study guide text is coauthored by Ken Gire, a graduate of Texas Christian University and Dallas Theological Seminary. The Living Insights are written by Bill Butterworth, a graduate of Florida Bible College, Dallas Theological Seminary, and Florida Atlantic University. Ken Gire is presently the director of educational products at Insight for Living, and Bill Butterworth is currently the director of counseling ministries.

Editor in Chief:	Cynthia Swindoll
Coauthor of Text:	Ken Gire
Author of Living Insights:	Bill Butterworth
Assistant Editor:	Karene Wells
Copy Manager:	Jac La Tour
Senior Copy Editor:	Jane Gillis
Copy Editor:	Glenda Schlahta
Director, Communications Division:	Carla Beck
Project Manager:	Nina Paris
Project Supervisor:	Cassandra Lovato
Art Director:	Donna Mayo
Production Artist:	Diana Vasquez
Typographer:	Bob Haskins
Calligrapher:	David Aquistapace
Cover:	Painting by Carl Bloch, *Come Unto Me*, courtesy of Sofia Ambertina Church, Landskrona, Sweden
Print Production Manager:	Deedee Snyder
Printer:	Frye and Smith

Unless otherwise identified, all Scripture references are from the New American Standard Bible, © The Lockman Foundation 1960, 1962, 1963, 1968, 1971, 1972, 1973, 1975, 1977. Used by permission.

ISBN 0-8499-8295-2

Ordering Information

An album that contains twelve messages on six cassettes and corresponds to this study guide may be purchased through Insight for Living, Post Office Box 4444, Fullerton, California 92634. For ordering information and a current catalog, please write our office or call (714) 870-9161.

Canadian residents may obtain a catalog and ordering information through Insight for Living Ministries, Post Office Box 2510, Vancouver, British Columbia, Canada V6B 3W7, (604) 272-5811. Australian residents should direct their correspondence to Insight for Living Ministries, General Post Office Box 2823 EE, Melbourne, Victoria 3001. Other overseas residents should direct their correspondence to our Fullerton office.

If you wish to order by Visa or MasterCard, you are welcome to use our toll-free number, (800) 772-8888, Monday through Friday, between the hours of 8:30 A.M. and 4:00 P.M., Pacific time. This number may be used anywhere in the United States except Alaska, California, and Hawaii. Orders from these areas can be made by calling our general office number, (714) 870-9161. Orders from Canada can be made by calling (604) 272-5811.

Table of Contents

"That You May Believe" 1

Prelude to Deity 9

A Man Sent from God 16

Five Who Followed in Faith 24

Wine ... Coins ... and Signs 32

Brainstorming the New Birth 39

The Preacher Who Lost His Congregation 47

Water for a Thirsty Woman 53

Healing at a Distance 61

An Exposé of Legalism 68

The Claims of the Christ 76

Witnesses for the Defense 83

Books for Probing Further 92

Ordering Information/Order Form 95

Exalting Christ . . .
The Son of God

A Study of John 1–5

Jesus Christ is God! These four words state the theme of John's Gospel. They also convey the underlying message of his first five chapters. His hope is to convince his readers of the undiminished deity of the Son of God. To miss that fact is to miss the message of this fourth book of the New Testament.

These studies are designed to take us back to the first century . . . to clear away all the debris of traditional opinions and personal feelings so that we are able to examine the evidence. When we do, we shall realize that Jesus of Nazareth was, in fact, truly God.

May our Lord use these studies to convince you of His lordship, His majesty, His authority. And as He does, let us exalt His name together.

Chuck Swindoll

Putting Truth into Action

Knowledge apart from application falls short of God's desire for His children. Knowledge must result in change and growth. Consequently, we have constructed this Bible study guide with these purposes in mind: (1) to stimulate discovery, (2) to increase understanding, and (3) to encourage application.

At the end of each lesson is a section called 🖼️ **Living Insights.** *There you'll be given assistance in further Bible study, and you'll be encouraged to contemplate and apply the things you've learned. This is the place where the lesson is fitted with shoe leather for your walk through the varied experiences of life.*

It's our hope that you'll discover numerous ways to use this tool. Some useful avenues we suggest are personal meditation, joint discovery, and discussion with your spouse, family, work associates, friends, or neighbors. The study guide is also practical for Sunday school classes, Bible study groups, and, of course, as a study aid for the "Insight for Living" radio broadcast.

In order to derive the greatest benefit from this process, we suggest that you record your responses to the lessons in the space which has been provided for you. In view of the kinds of questions asked, your study guide may become a journal filled with your many discoveries and commitments. We anticipate that you will find yourself returning to it periodically for review and encouragement.

Ken Gire
Coauthor of Text

Bill Butterworth
Author of Living Insights

Exalting Christ... The Son of God

A STUDY OF JOHN 1–5

"That You May Believe"

Survey of John

Before we cross the threshold of John's Gospel, we are compelled to take off our shoes, for every page is ablaze with deity. More than with almost any other book, we realize that here we are standing on holy ground.

For many Christian people the Gospel according to *St. John* is the most precious book in the New Testament. It is the book on which above all they feed their minds and nourish their hearts, and in which they rest their souls. Very often on stained glass windows and the like the gospel writers are represented in symbol by the figures of the four beasts whom the writer of the *Revelation* saw around the throne (*Revelation* 4:7). The emblems are variously distributed among the gospel writers, but a common allocation is that . . . the *eagle* stands for *John,* because it alone of all living creatures can look straight into the sun and not be dazzled, and John has the most penetrating gaze of all the New Testament writers into the eternal mysteries and the eternal truths and the very mind of God. Many people find themselves closer to God and to Jesus Christ in *John* than in any other book in the world.[1]

I. Background of John's Gospel

John writes with a simple, straightforward style. Seldom will you find a word over three syllables; most are one or two—"In the beginning was the Word, and the Word was with God, and the Word was God" (John 1:1). Simple . . . straightforward . . . yet sublime. John is also a writer fond of contrasts. Light and dark. Life and death. Spirit and flesh. A story may jump from sadness to ecstasy, from stormy conflict to the sweetest calm, from a crisis of doubt to concrete assurance. Another aspect of John's style is that he does not use a running video camera to record the life of Jesus. Rather, he uses a more selective snapshot approach. Consequently, John reads more like a

---

1. William Barclay, *The Gospel of John*, vol. 1, rev. ed. (Edinburgh, Scotland: Saint Andrew Press, 1975), p. 1.

thematic scrapbook of Christ's life than a meticulously chronicled documentary.

A. Why are there four Gospels? Why not one definitive biography of Christ rather than four separate accounts? Because a picture is more complete when taken from several different angles. Take sports, for example. The player, the coach, the referee, the fans, and the television cameras all look at a play from different angles. In order to get the fullest possible picture of the play, all angles have to be taken into consideration. Or take another example. The biography of a famous man is not really complete unless we have accounts from all perspectives—from his parents, mate, children, and so forth. Each would see things from a different viewpoint and thus give us a little different slant on his life. The parents would see him as son; the wife, as sweetheart; the children, as Daddy. Similarly, each Gospel writer looks at Jesus from his own distinct angle.[2]

1. **Matthew.** Matthew, writing to the Jews, was interested in establishing the regal rights of Jesus as King of the Jews. In doing so, he traced the genealogy of Jesus back to David and Abraham. He set forth Christ as the Redeemer-King of Israel, the Messiah promised to the forefathers. The inscription "Behold, your king" (Zech. 9:9) could be written over Matthew's Gospel, summarizing his view of Jesus.

2. **Mark.** Mark, writing to the Romans, was interested in capturing those shots of Jesus that showed Him as a servant. Consequently, we have no genealogy in Mark's Gospel; after all, who is interested in the lineage of a lowly servant? What Mark had his eye on was the *activity* of Jesus, which would appeal to a practical Roman citizen. Over Mark's Gospel the inscription might read "Behold, My Servant" (Isa. 42:1; compare Zech. 3:8).

3. **Luke.** Luke was writing primarily to a Greek audience and focused on Jesus' humanity. Consequently, Luke traced Christ's genealogy all the way back to Adam. Throughout his account, Luke pictured the Son of man as Kinsman-Redeemer to the whole human race, as one who was willing to save men of every nation. Over his Gospel we might inscribe "Behold, a man" (Zech. 6:12).

4. **John.** John wrote to a timeless, universal audience. More than the other writers, he stressed the deity of Christ and

2. Helpful books on reconciling the different Gospel accounts are: *A Harmony of the Gospels,* by Robert L. Thomas and Stanley N. Gundry (Chicago, Ill.: Moody Press, 1979); *A Guide to the Gospels,* by W. Graham Scroggie (Old Tappan, N.J.: Fleming H. Revell Co., 1967); *The Words and Works of Jesus Christ: A Study of the Life of Christ,* by J. Dwight Pentecost (Grand Rapids, Mich.: Zondervan Publishing House, 1981).

His unique relationship with the Father. Over his Gospel the words "Behold, your God" (Isa. 35:4) could be written in letters of gold.

Ecce Homo

Stop here and take a few minutes to "behold" Jesus.[3] Look at Him from every angle. He is the true king. He is the servant par excellence. He is the quintessential man—all that humanity was created to be. And He is God. Jesus Christ never changes. He is the same yesterday, today, and forever (Heb. 13:8).

Yet what we need Him to be at a given moment does change. There are times we need to realize that He is king and we are the subjects of His kingdom—times when we need Him to rule firmly and decisively in our lives. In other moments, however, we need Him to wash our feet and teach us, by example, how we are to serve others. Sometimes, we need to realize that He was once one of us, that He hungered and hurt, and that He sympathizes with our weaknesses. And there are times in our lives when we need to see Him as God, Creator and Sustainer of the universe, who is in control of our circumstances.

Hold Him up to the light. See every facet of His being sparkle. He is without flaw. Truly, a beautiful Savior!

B. Why do we have John's Gospel? John's Gospel differs significantly from the other three.[4] No account of Jesus' birth, baptism, or temptation is given. John tells nothing of the Last Supper, Gethsemane, or the Ascension. No word of the healing of any people possessed by devils or evil spirits is found in this Gospel. And, most surprisingly, it documents none of the parables. However, it does contain much that the others omit. John alone tells us of the wedding feast at Cana (2:1–11); of Nicodemus (3:1–15); of the woman at the well (chap. 4); of the raising of Lazarus (chap. 11); of Jesus washing the disciples' feet (13:1–17); of the teaching about the Holy Spirit as the divine Comforter

3. *Ecce homo* is Latin for "Behold, the Man!" taken from the Vulgate version of Pilate's words when he presented Jesus to the people before the Crucifixion (John 19:5).

4. The accounts of Matthew, Mark, and Luke are commonly referred to as the *synoptic* Gospels, from the words *sun* and *opsis* meaning "seeing together." To examine the differences between the synoptic accounts and John, consult *The Gospel of John,* by G. H. C. Macgregor (London, England: Hodder and Stoughton, n.d.), pp. x–xx.

(chaps. 14–17). Also unique to John are the vignettes of Thomas (11:16, 14:5, 20:24–29), Andrew (1:40–41, 6:8–9, 12:22), and Philip (6:5–7, 14:8–9). But beyond filling in missing snapshots to the scrapbook, John shows Jesus in the full light of His deity more than any of the other writers.

II. Overview of John's Gospel

Traditionally, the author of the Fourth Gospel has been almost unanimously viewed as John, the son of Zebedee and brother of James (Mark 1:19). Prior to becoming a disciple, he was in the fishing business with his brother and Peter (Luke 5:10). Along with Peter and James, he was part of the inner circle of disciples who were allowed to accompany Jesus on certain great occasions (Mark 5:37, 9:2, 14:33). Throughout the book of John he is distinguished as the closest person to Christ, the disciple whom Jesus loved (John 13:23, 19:26, 20:2).[5]

A. What is John's motive? John's underlying motive or purpose is explicitly stated in chapter 20.

> Many other signs therefore Jesus also performed in the presence of the disciples, which are not written in this book; but these have been written that you may believe that Jesus is the Christ, the Son of God; and that believing you may have life in His name. (vv. 30–31)

In a word, John was *selective* in the way he recorded the life of Christ. His purpose was to so screen and so structure his material that the narrative would lead the reader to the irrefutable conclusion that Jesus was indeed the Son of God (see 1:34, 49; 6:69; 10:36; 11:4, 27; 20:28, 31). And having led them to the Son, he would have them drink the living water that Jesus offers to all through faith (4:14). *Believe* is one of John's favorite words, used ninety-eight times in his Gospel. It is an active word, meaning "to depend upon" or "to trust."[6]

B. What is John's method? How does John go about presenting the evidence about Jesus so as to elicit our belief? Look again at 20:30–31 and you will see the clue.

---

5. The author of the Fourth Gospel is to be distinguished from John the Baptist (mentioned in John 1:6–8), who was not only related to Jesus (Luke 1:36) but also the forerunner to His ministry (Luke 1:13–17, Matt. 3). For an exhaustive discussion of the authorship of the Fourth Gospel, consult *The Gospel of John,* by William Hendrickson (London, England: Banner of Truth Trust, 1954), pp. 3–31.

6. The Greek word is *pisteuō;* the Hebrew, *aman.* In nontheological passages the root refers to a nurse, a master craftsman, a pillar, or even a doorpost (2 Kings 18:1b)—each of which must be depended upon for support. This same sense of dependence is captured in Proverbs 3:5, "Trust in the Lord with all your heart,/And do not lean on your own understanding." To trust God is to lean on Him—depend upon Him to hold us up—much the same way we trust that a chair will support us when we sit in it.

Many other *signs* therefore Jesus also performed in the presence of the disciples, which are not written in this book; but *these* have been written that you may believe that Jesus is the Christ, the Son of God; and that believing you may have life in His name. (emphasis added)

The word *sign*[7] refers to an act or miracle that is pregnant with meaning. It is not simply a display of supernatural power but a dynamic way of pointing out some aspect of the person of Christ. John records seven such signs, each a concrete demonstration that Jesus is God. These seven miracles all occur in Christ's *public ministry*, which lasts three years (chaps. 1–12). However, as public unbelief intensifies, the miracles cease, and for the few days before His Crucifixion, Jesus withdraws to a *private ministry* with the disciples (chaps. 13–21). John strategically places several keys to the structure of his Gospel where the attentive reader won't miss them. For example, one key, which we have already examined, is found in 20:30–31. A second key to understanding the structure of this book is found in verses 11–12 of chapter 1:

He came to His own, and those who were His own
did not receive Him. But as many as received Him,
to them He gave the right to become children of God,
even to those who believe in His name.

"He came to his own" corresponds to chapters 1–12, meaning that Jesus appeared first to His chosen people, the Jews. "And those who were His own did not receive Him" parallels chapters 13–19, depicting how these rightful heirs forfeited their birthright by rejecting their Savior. "But as many as received Him, to them He gave the right to become children of God, even to those who believe in His name" coincides with chapters 20–21. In these final chapters, God accepts the Gentiles as His children and heirs.[8]

A Concluding Application

From Shakespeare to Solzhenitsyn, the words of great writers reach across centuries and continents to grace us with the warm touch of kindness, the delicate touch of beauty, and the firm touch of truth. The Gospel of John is one of those books. It is not an exhaustive account of Christ's life. By his own admission John writes:

---

7. The Greek word is *sēmeion*.

8. John 16:28 gives yet a third outline of the book: Chapters 1–12 are summarized in the sentence " 'I came forth from the Father, and have come into the world.' " Chapters 13–19 are included in Christ's next statement, " 'I am leaving the world again.' " And He prepares the disciples for His departure in chapters 20–21 with " 'and [I am] going to the Father.' "

And there are also many other things which
Jesus did, which if they were written in detail,
I suppose that even the world itself would not
contain the books which were written. (21:25)
John's intent is not to write an epic on the life of Christ
but to hold Jesus up so we can see His glorious light and
come out of the darkness. And when all is said and done,
could there be a piece of literature with a more noble or
eternal purpose? As C. S. Lewis stated:
But the Christian knows from the outset that
the salvation of a single soul is more important
than the production or preservation of all the
epics and tragedies in the world.[9]
What kind of things do you read? Sizzling best-sellers . . .
the *Wall Street Journal* . . . *People* magazine? They may
keep you enthralled, informed, and entertained, but none
of them offer you what John has to offer. As we start our
series on the Gospel of John, will you commit yourself to
making it a priority on your reading list? It will change
your life if you do—and that's a promise even Shakespeare
couldn't make!

Living Insights

Study One ━━━━━━━━━━━━━━━━━━━━━━━━━━━━━━━━━━━

"But these have been written that you may believe that Jesus is the
Christ, the Son of God; and that believing you may have life in His
name" (John 20:31). In that simple statement, the apostle John tells us
what this historical account is all about. It's always exciting to embark
on an adventure of this nature. Let's sneak a peek at where we will be
going in the studies ahead.

● Let's get an overview of the Gospel of John. Depending on how much
time you have, casually acquaint yourself with these twenty-one
chapters. If time is short, skim the text briefly. If you have more time,
though, read with greater care. Consult the outline of the book that
follows this lesson. It should aid you in seeing the order and progres-
sion in the writing.

9. C. S. Lewis, "Christianity and Literature," *Christian Reflections* (Grand Rapids, Mich.: William B.
Eerdmans Publishing Co., 1968), p. 10.

📖 Living Insights

The study of John's Gospel is a major undertaking. It will not be accomplished in a short period of time. Rather, it requires a long-term commitment. Let's take a few minutes to get our priorities in order before going any further in this study. Think through the following questions.

- Will I commit myself to faithfully study John's Gospel?
- When will I schedule it into my routine?
- Is there someone to whom I could be accountable during this study?
- Am I willing to allow God to change my life through these lessons?

John: The Book That Helps Us Believe

One phrase that describes the book:
"that you may believe that
Jesus is . . . the Son of God"

Two roads that traverse the book:
Belief—disciples trained
and strengthened
Unbelief—people's rejection

Three keys that unlock the book:
Front door (1:11–12)
Side door (16:28)
Back door (20:30–31)

Four terms that fill the book:
Believe (98 times)
World (78 times)
Know (55 times)
Glorify (42 times)

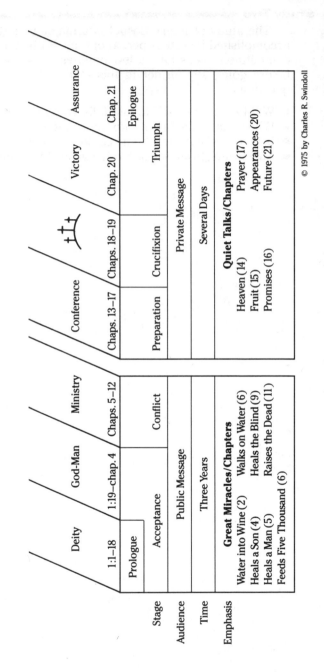

Stage	Deity	God-Man	Ministry	Conference		Victory	Assurance
	1:1–18	1:19–chap. 4	Chaps. 5–12	Chaps. 13–17	Chaps. 18–19	Chap. 20	Chap. 21
	Prologue	Acceptance	Conflict	Preparation	Crucifixion	Triumph	Epilogue
Audience		Public Message			Private Message		
Time		Three Years			Several Days		

Great Miracles/Chapters
Water into Wine (2)   Walks on Water (6)
Heals a Son (4)   Heals the Blind (9)
Heals a Man (5)   Raises the Dead (11)
Feeds Five Thousand (6)

Quiet Talks/Chapters
Heaven (14)   Prayer (17)
Fruit (15)   Appearances (20)
Promises (16)   Future (21)

Prelude to Deity
John 1:1–18

In his classic *A Tale of Two Cities,* Charles Dickens summarizes the era of the French Revolution.

It was the best of times, it was the worst of times, it was the age of wisdom, it was the age of foolishness, it was the epoch of belief, it was the epoch of incredulity, it was the season of Light, it was the season of Darkness, it was the spring of hope, it was the winter of despair, we had everything before us, we had nothing before us, we were all going direct to Heaven, we were all going direct the other way.[1]

With this prologue Dickens preludes his drama. Before the curtain rises, he introduces us to some of the novel's major themes—prosperity and poverty, light and darkness, hope and despair.

John also introduces his Gospel with a prologue. R. C. H. Lenski, in his commentary on the Gospel of John, sees this eighteen-verse introduction as some of the most scintillating writing in the entire New Testament.

John's is the paragon among the Gospels, "the one, tender, real crown-Gospel of them all" (Luther), and the prolog is the central jewel set in pure gold.[2]

Like Dickens's introduction, John's prologue gives us a glimmer of the book's major themes: the deity of Christ; Christ as light and life; the world shrouded in darkness; the witness of John the Baptist; Israel's rejection of their Savior; Gentile acceptance; and examples of the glory, grace, and truth of Christ.

In this prologue, John establishes five arguments as to why Jesus was, in fact, divine: He was eternal (vv. 1–2); He was the Creator (vv. 3–5, 9); He gave spiritual life (vv. 10–13); He manifested glory (vv. 14–17); and He explained God (v. 18). Turning, then, to chapter 1, we will examine in depth John's *prelude to deity.*

I. The Son of God in Eternity

Alluding to the Creation account in Genesis 1:1, John establishes the deity of Christ by giving us a glimpse of Him before the foundation of the earth.

In the beginning was the Word, and the Word was with God, and the Word was God. (John 1:1)

---

1. Charles Dickens, *A Tale of Two Cities* (Garden City, N.Y.: Nelson Doubleday, n.d.), p. 9.

2. R. C. H. Lenski, *The Interpretation of St. John's Gospel* (Columbus, Ohio: Wartburg Press, 1942), p. 26.

As we step into John's Gospel, we immediately slide through a time tunnel that transports us to eternity past. In eternity—before man, before creation, before time itself—there existed the everlasting, triune God.

Lord, Thou hast been our dwelling place in all generations.
Before the mountains were born,
Or Thou didst give birth to the earth and the world,
Even from everlasting to everlasting, Thou art God.
(Ps. 90:1–2)

John introduces Jesus as "the Word." Words communicate, and that's precisely what Jesus did. Like a capstone to the pyramid of prophets that preceded Him, Jesus was the final spokesman for God (Heb. 1:1–2). From A to Z, Jesus was the divine alphabet spelling out God in such a way that even the most elementary of us could grasp His essence (Rev. 1:8). This Word, John reveals to us, was *with* God, face-to-face, in eternity past. Yet in some mysterious way, this Word was not only with God but *was* God. Jesus was not simply the revealer of God but God Himself revealed.

The Divine Word

Words have a way of galvanizing us into action. In the days of the French Revolution Rouget de Lisle wrote the *Marseillaise* and that song sent men marching to revolution. The words did things. In the days of the Second World War, when Britain was bereft alike of allies and of weapons, the words of the Prime Minister, Sir Winston Churchill, as he broadcast to the nation, did things to people.[3]

How about you? Is the divine Word sending chills down your back and stirring your heart? Or is He simply going in one ear and out the other?

II. The Son of God at Creation

Verses 2–3 expand on the Son's role in creation.

He was in the beginning with God. All things came into being by Him, and apart from Him nothing came into being that has come into being.

Two salient facts regarding Christ's deity are expressed here: (1) Christ Himself was not created, and (2) all things were created by Him. The Father was the architect, but Jesus was the primary agent of

---

3. William Barclay, *The Gospel of John,* vol. 1, rev. ed. (Edinburgh, Scotland: Saint Andrew Press, 1975), p. 28.

creation (see also v. 10). First Corinthians 8:6 supports this divine division of labor.

Yet for us there is but one God, the Father, from whom are all things, and we exist for Him; and one Lord, Jesus Christ, by whom are all things, and we exist through Him.

Picking up on this idea, Colossians 1:16–17 reveals that Jesus is not only the Creator of the universe but its Sustainer as well.

For by Him all things were created, both in the heavens and on earth, visible and invisible, whether thrones or dominions or rulers or authorities—all things have been created by Him and for Him. And He is before all things, and in Him all things hold together.

In verses 4–5, John tells us something of the nature of this divine Word.

In Him was life, and the life was the light of men. And the light shines in the darkness, and the darkness did not comprehend it.

Behind Christ's creative involvement was one crucial and dynamic element: life! Turning from Christ's creative work to His saving work, John shows us that just as Christ is the source of all physical life, so is He also the source of all spiritual life.

The Meaning of Life

Macbeth, in Shakespeare's play of the same name, reveals his philosophy of life.

Life's but a walking shadow, a poor player
That struts and frets his hour upon the stage
And then is heard no more. It is a tale
Told by an idiot, full of sound and fury,
Signifying nothing.[4]

However, in John's drama, life is not summed up in a philosophy but in a person: "In *Him* was life, and the life was the light of men" (v. 4, emphasis added).

If you're looking for the essence of life in a philosophy, you'll go away empty-handed. But if you come to the person of Christ, you will find that *He* is life (14:6), and you'll walk away with your arms full of His abundance (10:10b).

Parenthetically, we are told of John the Baptist's ministry in relation to this life-giving light.

There came a man, sent from God, whose name was John. He came for a witness, that he might bear witness of the light, that all might believe through him. (vv. 6–7)

4. William Shakespeare, *Macbeth*, act 5, sc. 5, lines 24–28.

11

To prevent confusion, John distinguishes Jesus from His cousin John the Baptist by making clear each man's role: John as the messenger, Jesus as the Messiah.

He [John] was not the light, but came that he might bear witness of the light. There was the true light which, coming into the world, enlightens every man. (vv. 8–9)

Four things can be said of *light* in these verses: First, it originates with Christ (v. 4). Second, it is not overpowered by darkness (v. 5). Third, it is unique—the *true* light (v. 9a). Fourth, it is universally available—it enlightens *every* man (v. 9b). A public utility, like the electric company, offers its services to every home within its area. In the same way, Christ offers life to enlighten every heart that draws close to Him.

Lighting Up Your Life

Jesus is truly the light of the world. If you accept Him as your Savior, He can light up your life no matter how dark it may be.

For God, who said, "Light shall shine out of darkness," is the One who has shone in our hearts to give the light of the knowledge of the glory of God in the face of Christ. (2 Cor. 4:6)

Where there is chaos, He can bring order. Where there is emptiness, He can bring fullness. Where there is darkness, He can bring light. And the darkness—no matter how deep—cannot overpower it!

III. The Son of God on Earth

In spite of the fact that Jesus offers Himself to everyone without exception, His light is shunned by many.

He was in the world, and the world was made through Him, and the world did not know Him. He came to His own, and those who were His own did not receive Him. But as many as received Him, to them He gave the right to become children of God, even to those who believe in His name, who were born not of blood, nor of the will of the flesh, nor of the will of man, but of God. (vv. 10–13)

Like children coming out of a Saturday matinee—whose eyes squint at the light of day and who shrink back into the theater—many refused to step into the light of Christ (see 3:19). The world, in its hardness, stood as a defiant piece of sculpture, shunning its sculptor and refusing to acknowledge Christ as its maker. Not only did the creation "not know Him" (v. 10), but even Jesus' own people, the Jews, "did not receive Him" (v. 11). Fortunately, however, some did:

a Samaritan woman here (chap. 4), an adulterous woman there (chap. 8), a lone blind man (chap. 9), and so on. Candle by candle, Jesus touched these dimly burning wicks of downtrodden humanity; and wick by wick, they, in turn, became lights to a world shivering in darkness (see Matt. 5:14–16).

IV. The Son of God Incarnate
Verse 14 describes the Incarnation—God becoming man in the person of Christ.[5]

> And the Word became flesh, and dwelt[6] among us, and
> we beheld His glory, glory as of the only begotten from
> the Father, full of grace and truth.

In the Incarnation, deity funneled itself into humanity—the finest of wines into an ordinary earthenware vessel. Jesus traveled throughout Judea, Samaria, and Galilee as a common, unglazed earthenware bottle, corked until those special occasions when His glory was manifested and the fragrant bouquet of deity filled the air with its aromatic presence. And, for a fleeting but festive moment, the world's parched lips tasted of the kingdom of God. Of this glorious Savior John the Baptist testified.

> John bore witness of Him, and cried out, saying, "This was
> He of whom I said, 'He who comes after me has higher
> rank than I, for He existed before me.' " For of His fulness
> we have all received, and grace upon grace. For the Law
> was given through Moses; grace and truth were realized
> through Jesus Christ. (vv. 15–17)

Like a fountain fills the cups of eager street children, Jesus fills us from His bottomless reservoir of grace and truth until at last our cups overflow.

V. The Son of God Explained the Father
When the divine sculptor became human clay, the abstractions of deity were explained in very concrete, human terms.

> No man has seen God at any time; the only begotten God,
> who is in the bosom of the Father, He has explained Him.
> (v. 18)

Jesus explained God.[7] He was "the image of the invisible God" (Col. 1:15), "the exact representation of His nature" (Heb. 1:3). On

---

5. See also Philippians 2:5–8.

6. Literally, *tabernacled.* This is a latent reference to the tabernacle of Israel in the wilderness. The tabernacle was a temporary place where man could meet with God. It was humble in its external appearance, but inside dwelt the *Shekinah* glory. For an interesting discussion of this, consult Arthur W. Pink's *Exposition of the Gospel of John* (Grand Rapids, Mich.: Zondervan Publishing House, 1970), pp. 34–41.

7. Literally, *exegeted,* meaning "to draw out, to expound, to explain."

this climactic note, John ends his prologue. He has carefully presented his evidence and shown that this Jesus of Nazareth, this carpenter's son, could be none other than the Son of God—because He's eternal (vv. 1–2), because He's the Creator (v. 3), because He's the source of life (vv. 4–13), because He's God's manifested glory (vv. 14–17), and because He's the unique explanation of God (v. 18).

Living Insights

With remarkable force and clarity, the apostle John brings his readers into the presence of the God of creation. The statements he makes about the Lord Jesus should not be taken lightly. Let's dig deeper into this great introductory text.

- John 1:1–18 is rich with marvelous statements about the Son of God. Using the chart provided for you, list what this passage tells about the Lord Jesus. Remember, no observation is too small or too simple ... each one is important.

The Lord Jesus Christ	
Verses	Observations

Verses	Observations

 Living Insights

Study Two ▬▬▬▬▬▬▬▬▬▬▬▬▬▬▬▬▬▬▬

Now that we know some facts about the Gospel of John, let's discuss how they affect us. Get together with a group of family members or friends and use the following statements as conversation starters. As you delve into the Scriptures, encourage open and frank comments.

• According to the first three verses of John, our Savior created everything—and that, of course, includes you. Take some time to talk about how God has made each person in your group. Share with each other the differences He has given you and how they enhance your group.
• Read verses 10–13. Why didn't the world know Jesus? Who were "His own"? What does it mean to receive Him or believe in His name? Share with one another how and when you accepted Him as your personal Savior.
• As you read verses 16–17, think about God's grace. Can you define it? Can you illustrate it? Why is it better than the Law? Does it have limitations?

A Man Sent from God

John 1:6–8, 15, 19–34

More than five hundred years ago, in the little hamlet of Ferrara, Italy, a baby boy was born into a physician's home. His parents named him Girolamo Savonarola. Little did they realize that their baby would grow up to be a man sent from God.

From his earliest years, this keen, intelligent boy possessed an invincible love for God. By his own testimony, he was prepared to abandon life itself for the glory of Christ.

His saintly life was a mixture of loneliness and ruggedness. He deprived himself of every indulgence, content with only the hardest couch, the roughest clothing, the plainest food.

Savonarola lived in a time characterized by corruption and wickedness among the papacy, the priesthood, and the entire clergy. The offices of bishop and cardinal were put up for auction and sold to the highest bidder. Immorality in its grossest forms was prevalent in monasteries and convents; even in local congregations it was displayed without shame. The church had become a den of vice and iniquity.

This so burdened the young priest that he spoke with fiery eloquence against these practices. For eight years he preached at the cathedral in Florence, pleading for purity of life and simplicity of worship.

Refusing to mix and mingle with officials of the church, he was resented and publicly assaulted by the clergy. Martyrdom appeared inevitable. Interrupting his devotions, church leaders broke into his monastery, dragged him into the streets, and locked him away in a loathsome dungeon. There he was tortured for weeks.

Finally, the day of his trial came. The church leaders were so determined to destroy him that one of the pope's commissioners wrote: " 'Put Savonarola to death, even if he were another John the Baptist.' "[1]

In a fit of unjust rage, they hanged him, set fire to his remains, and threw his ashes into the river Arno.

In Savonarola we find a perfect parallel to John the Baptist. Savonarola was a man sent from God to Italy; John the Baptist was a man sent from God to Israel. Both lived modestly and preached mightily. And both were forerunners, paving a highway for their Lord in a moral wilderness: Savonarola for the Reformation; John the Baptist for the kingdom of God.

1. Philip Schaff, *History of the Christian Church,* vol. 6 (Grand Rapids, Mich.: William B. Eerdmans Publishing Co., 1910), p. 710. For further study on Savonarola's life, consult pages 684–716 of the same volume.

I. Background of the Man Sent

John's parents were Zacharias and Elizabeth, both older people, neither of whom expected to have a baby (Luke 1:7). Luke informs us that from his boyhood until the day of his public ministry John lived in the deserts (1:80). During this time, he was clothed in camel's hair, wore a leather belt, and ate a steady diet of locusts and wild honey (Mark 1:6). He gave a fire-and-brimstone call to repentance in order to prepare the way for Jesus (Matt. 3).

II. Characteristics of the Man Sent

Although his name was the most common of names, the man himself was the most uncommon of men.

A. He was human, but not ordinary. John 1:6 reveals a lot about this extraordinary man.

> There came a man, sent from God, whose name was John.

John was no angel, no spark of divinity—just a man. There was nothing significant about his name, unlike the names Immanuel and Jesus that were fraught with meaning. He was just John in a plain brown wrapper . . . but he was not ordinary. He stood virtually alone and fit into no preformed mold. He was neither Pharisee nor Sadducee nor priest nor Levite nor scribe. He didn't look like a prophet, didn't sound like a priest, and didn't smell like a saint.

B. He was a lamp, but not the light. Verse 7 tell us precisely why John came.

> He came for a witness, that he might bear witness of the light, that all might believe through him.

John came as a witness[2] with one goal in mind: to turn people around so they could see the light. His was not an office embellished with the trappings of pomp and ceremony. He was no religious dignitary or published theologian. He was simply a beggar telling other beggars where to find bread, as verse 8 indicates.

> He was not the light, but came that he might bear witness of the light.

John was a lamp, but not the light; a wick, but not the flame. The "true light" that enlightens every man was Jesus (v. 9). Consequently, John saw himself in the shadow of the Savior.

---

2. The Greek noun for *witness* is *marturia;* the verb form is *martureō.* It means "to testify, to affirm the truth about someone or something." The context is centered around John's teaching. Of the thirty-seven instances of the noun, thirty are found in John's writings; of the seventy-six instances of the verb, forty-seven are found in John's writings. From this Greek root, we get our word *martyr,* which means "a person who chooses to suffer or die rather than give up his faith or principles." Such turned out to be the case for John the Baptist (Matt. 14:1–12).

John bore witness of Him, and cried out, saying, "This was He of whom I said, 'He who comes after me has a higher rank than I, for He existed before me.' " (v. 15)

Some Personal Application

Most of us have had a variety of lamps in our homes over the years: desk lamps, swag lamps, chandeliers. Some have probably been fancy, fashioned in brass or silver. Some have been made of stained glass; others, crystal. Some, too, may have been very common, like a simple porcelain closet fixture.

Whatever, the important thing is the light, not the lamp. It's the glow in the bulb that lights up a room, not the shine on the brass or crystal.

Are you exhibiting Christ in your life as the true light of the world, or is the ornamentation of your lamp the main thing people see? Is His light radiating through your life, or is it being obstructed by a cumbersome lampshade of sin?

C. He was a voice, but not the Word. Like the relationship between a singer's voice and the song's lyrics, John was simply "a voice crying in the wilderness" (v. 23), while Jesus was the Word of God (vv. 1–2).

And this is the witness of John, when the Jews sent to him priests and Levites from Jerusalem to ask him, "Who are you?" And he confessed, and did not deny, and he confessed, "I am not the Christ." And they asked him, "What then? Are you Elijah?"[3] And he said, "I am not." "Are you the Prophet?"[4] And he answered, "No." They said then to him, "Who are you, so that we may give an answer to those who sent us? What do you say about yourself?" He said, "I am a voice of one crying in the wilderness, 'Make straight the way of the Lord,' as Isaiah the prophet said." (vv. 19–23)

3. Malachi predicted that Elijah would come to herald the appearance of the Messiah (Mal. 4:5). The synoptic writers persistently identified John with Elijah (Matt. 11:14, 17:12; Mark 9:11–13), which poses a problem in light of John's denial in verse 21. However, the problem is resolved when it is understood that John is denying a *physical* identification with Elijah, while the synoptic writers are *spiritually* identifying John with the prophet. Compare the angel of the Lord's words about John in Luke 1:17: " 'And it is he who will go as a forerunner before Him *in the spirit and power* of Elijah . . .' " (emphasis added).

4. See Deuteronomy 18:15.

Why did one have to make straight the way of the Lord? What did John mean by these words? The quote is from Isaiah 40:3, and the imagery is explained by Merrill Tenney in his commentary on John's Gospel.

The imagery was taken from the days when there were no paved roads, only tracks across the fields. If a king were to travel, the road must be built and smoothed out that the royal chariot might not find the traveling unduly rough, nor be swamped in the mire.[5]

Just as a special road had to be leveled when a king desired to cross a desert, so a path was to be paved by John for the Messiah.

Highway through the Heart

To describe Israel's spiritual condition at the coming of the Messiah, John chooses the metaphor of a wilderness—a place that is desolate, dry, and barren. What metaphor would he be inclined to choose if he had to describe your heart? Would it be a wilderness ... a fallow field ... a meadow ... or an Eden?

The highway to heaven is paved over prepared hearts. Hearts that are repentant. Hearts that are soft. Hearts that are fertile. Isaiah makes it clear that the rough terrain in our hearts needs to be smoothed before the Lord can come near.

A voice is calling,
"Clear the way for the Lord in the wilderness;
Make smooth in the desert a highway for our
    God.
Let every valley be lifted up,
And every mountain and hill be made low;
And let the rough ground become a plain,
And the rugged terrain a broad valley."
(Isa. 40:3–4)

When you read your Bible and pray, have you first cleared the way for the Lord in the wilderness of your heart? When you worship, have you first made smooth in the desert a highway for your God? If God seems distant in your life, maybe you need to do a little roadwork of repentance in order to prepare the way for Him.

---

5. Merrill C. Tenney, *John: The Gospel of Belief* (Grand Rapids, Mich.: William B. Eerdmans Publishing Co., 1948), p. 79.

D. He was useful, but not indispensable. Still confused, those sent by the Pharisees probed further.

And they asked him, and said to him, "Why then are you baptizing, if you are not the Christ, nor Elijah, nor the Prophet?" John answered them saying, "I baptize in water, but among you stands One whom you do not know. It is He who comes after me, the thong of whose sandal I am not worthy to untie." These things took place in Bethany beyond the Jordan, where John was baptizing. (vv. 25–28)

John's humility can readily be seen in verse 27, but the background to the verse brings it into even sharper focus. There is a rabbinic saying that John probably had in mind when he spoke of Jesus' sandal. " 'Every service which a slave performs for his master shall a disciple do for his teacher except the loosing of his sandalthong.' "6 John was willing to stoop to the lowest level of servility in deference to the Messiah.

E. He was a witness, but not an object of worship. A witness does not tell his own story but testifies only to what he has seen and heard. In verses 29–33, John gave his testimony regarding Jesus.

The next day he saw Jesus coming to him, and said, "Behold, the Lamb of God who takes away the sin of the world! This is He on behalf of whom I said, 'After me comes a Man who has a higher rank than I, for He existed before me.' And I did not recognize Him, but in order that He might be manifested to Israel, I came baptizing in water." And John bore witness saying, "I have beheld the Spirit descending as a dove out of heaven, and He remained upon Him. And I did not recognize Him, but He who sent me to baptize in water said to me, 'He upon whom you see the Spirit descending and remaining upon Him, this is the one who baptizes in the Holy Spirit.' "

After all the evidence was in, John climactically announced his verdict.

"And I have seen, and have borne witness that this is the Son of God." (v. 34)

III. Marks of God-Sent People Today

Leadership has its own particular perils: pride, egotism, envy, jealousy, the compromises of popularity, assumed infallibility, illusions

---

6. Quoted by Leon Morris in *Commentary on the Gospel of John* (Grand Rapids, Mich.: William B. Eerdmans Publishing Co., 1971), p. 141.

of indispensability, and so on. But John gave a timeless principle for us in chapter 3, verse 30.

"He must increase, but I must decrease."

The true qualities of people sent by God are that they exalt the One who sent them, and they diminish the one who is sent.

Second Wind for Savonarola

Savonarola had an incredible experience when he went from Genoa to Florence. Believing that God had sent him to minister to the corrupt San Marco monastery, Savonarola journeyed there, only to collapse with fatigue at the base of the mountain range that led to the monastery.

Despairing of life, Savonarola was visited by a stranger. Whether the stranger was real or a vision or an angel, we don't know. But the story has the visitor feeding the discouraged traveler, giving him rest, and encouraging him.

The stranger helped Savonarola reach the gate of the monastery. Once there, the stranger is reported to have said, "And now, Savonarola, remember to do that for which God has sent thee;" then to have left.

Being a voice in a moral wilderness can be a lonely and discouraging experience. It's easy for fatigue and despair to set in. But many of you have felt the call to be that voice—in your family, at your school, where you work.

If that's the case, and you're feeling faint and discouraged . . . feeling you can't go on . . . I hope this study has given you some much-needed nourishment and rest. Now, let me be that stranger and encourage you to get up and "remember to do that for which God has sent thee."

Living Insights

Study One

In our last study, we concentrated on characteristics of Christ. But, as you were completing that exercise, you surely noticed another name appearing frequently. Let's look at that *other* person . . . the man sent from God named John.

- The chart on the following page is like the one in our previous lesson, except that this study asks for observations on John the Baptist. In this chart we will use the same chapter, the same strategy for study, the same goal. It will be interesting to notice the *relationship* between Christ and John the Baptist as you work through this text.

A Man Sent from God	
Verses	Observations

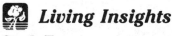 *Living Insights*

John the Baptist was no ordinary guy, even in his time. But can you imagine how he would look if he were alive in our day? How would people perceive him? Would his message be accepted or rejected? How would *you* relate to him?

- With the help of your God-given imagination, write a modern-day account of the story of John the Baptist. Place him in your town, in your time, with your friends and acquaintances—and, oh yes, with you too. You may be surprised at what you discover about this man and the relationships he might have developed had he lived in our day.

A Man Sent from God—Updated

_____

_____

_____

_____

_____

_____

_____

_____

_____

_____

_____

_____

_____

_____

_____

_____

_____

_____

Five Who Followed in Faith

John 1:35–51

Religious art has, for centuries, cast the disciples of Christ into porcelain molds—museum-quality reproductions, polished and protected. Glossed over with the smooth glaze of reverence, the flaws of the Twelve have largely been forgotten by time. But the people whom Jesus called were hardly porcelain-perfect saints.

The men and women to whom Jesus offered this gift were ordinary human beings, faulted and flawed, just like the rest of us. He gave his disciples no job descriptions; he did not disqualify Mary Magdalene because she had been afflicted with seven demons; he did not spend a lot of time looking for the most qualified people, the most adult. Instead, he chose people who were still childlike enough to leave the known comforts of the daily world, the security of their jobs, their reasonable way of life, to follow him.[1]

In this lesson, we will take a closer look at five of those men—five who followed in faith.

I. General Orientation

Let's survey the ground covered in the last half of John 1 before we look at each verse individually.

A. Time. This passage from John's daily diary describes a three-day period. Note the words "next day" repeated in verses 29, 35, and 43.

B. Structure. The passage is simple and straightforward in style, with a definite structure emerging from John's observation of each of the five men. In each case, there is an evangelistic approach, which creates interest, and then a conversation with Christ, which leads to a life-changing decision.

C. Characters. Only four are actually named: Andrew, Peter, Philip, and Nathanael. The fifth, cloaked in the authorial garb of anonymity, is John. All are ordinary, T-shirt-and-blue-jeans types—working men, primed for a challenge.

II. Specific Exposition

As we look at the calling of each disciple, we can see both similarities and differences in the way they came to follow Christ.

A. Andrew and John. The first men to follow Jesus were Andrew and John. The scene is staged to spotlight a transference of

---

1. Madeleine L'Engle, *Walking on Water: Reflections on Faith and Art* (Wheaton, Ill.: Harold Shaw Publishers, 1980), p. 89.

loyalty—from their old mentor, John the Baptist, to their new master, Jesus the Messiah.

> Again the next day John was standing with two of his disciples, and he looked upon Jesus as He walked, and said, "Behold, the Lamb of God!" And the two disciples heard him speak, and they followed Jesus. (vv. 35–37)

Notice the structure of the account: first the *approach* (v. 35), then the *message* (v. 36), and finally the *response* (v. 37). The approach was through mass evangelism. The message was that Jesus was "the Lamb of God."[2] The result—they followed Christ.

A Time to Reflect

In John Baillie's devotional classic, *A Diary of Private Prayer,* the author asks God to keep him "loyal to every hallowed memory of the past."[3]

Do you remember the time when you, like Andrew and John, first realized that Jesus was the sacrificial lamb who died in your place? Remember when you came to Him by faith and He embraced you with forgiveness? Angels rejoiced in heaven and you were given new life . . . a second chance . . . a fresh start for all eternity.

It may have been years ago, but you can probably still remember every detail of that day. Take a few minutes to reflect on that time and hallow that moment in your memory.

A more personal picture of these two fledgling disciples is folded away in verses 38–39.

> And Jesus turned, and beheld them following, and said to them, "What do you seek?" And they said to Him, "Rabbi (which translated means Teacher), where are You staying?" He said to them, "Come, and you will see." They came therefore and saw where He was staying; and they stayed with Him that day, for it was about the tenth hour.

With their whole world turned suddenly upside down, Andrew and John needed time alone with Jesus in order to rearrange their lives. With the question "What do you seek?" Jesus probed

---

2. The Passover lamb was a foreshadowing of Christ (compare Exod. 12 with 1 Cor. 5:7; also compare Isa. 53:7 with 1 Pet. 1:19). For a fuller discussion, consult Leon Morris, *The Word Was Made Flesh: John 1–5,* vol. 1 of *Reflections on the Gospel of John* (Grand Rapids, Mich.: Baker Book House, 1986), pp. 35–42.

3. John Baillie, *A Diary of Private Prayer* (New York, N.Y.: Charles Scribner's Sons, 1949), p. 9.

their motives. And with His invitation "Come, and you will see," He demonstrated His belief that their motives were pure. He graciously invited them to more intimate surroundings where their questions could be answered and their apprehensions resolved.

B. Simon Peter. What word comes to mind when you think of Simon Peter? Impulsive? Vocal? Intolerant? Perhaps all of these. Yet when Jesus met Simon, the word that came to His mind connoted an image both solid and stable—*Cephas,* the word for *stone*[4] (vv. 40–42).

> One of the two who heard John speak, and followed Him, was Andrew, Simon Peter's brother. He found first his own brother Simon, and said to him, "We have found the Messiah" (which translated means Christ). He brought him to Jesus. Jesus looked at him, and said, "You are Simon the son of John; you shall be called Cephas" (which translated means Peter).

Notice again the sequence of events. The approach was one of personal evangelism, brother to brother (vv. 40–41a). The message was "We have found the Messiah"[5] (v. 41b). The response was Peter's face-to-face encounter with Jesus, giving him the encouragement he needed to follow Christ (v. 42).

Seeing beyond the Rough Edges

Catching a glimpse of Peter's life under the magnifying glass of Scripture, we see a lot of rough edges on that stone. At times he is hardheaded, and at times, even abrasive.

But Jesus was able to see beyond all that—beyond the rough edges to the precious stone beneath, beyond the stubbornness to the stability.

Jesus had a jeweler's eye for spotting a diamond in the rough. Do you? Can you see the potential in others? Can you see beneath all the rough edges to the precious stone hidden within your child? Can you spot that jewel-in-the-making when you look at your mate or your friend?

---

4. See Irving L. Jensen, *John: A Self-Study Guide* (Chicago, Ill.: Moody Press, 1970), p. 32.

5. For the benefit of his non-Jewish readers, John translates the Hebrew term *Messiah* with the Greek *Christos* (from the root *chrio,* meaning "to anoint"). It means "the anointed one." "In the ancient world, . . . kings were anointed with oil at their coronation." William Barclay, *The Gospel of John,* vol. 1, rev. ed. (Edinburgh, Scotland: Saint Andrew Press, 1975), pp. 88–89.

> Oftentimes, a simple recognition of the presence of the jewel is all the encouragement people need to start chipping away at their own rough edges, bringing that precious stone to light.

C. Philip. Without John's record of several incidents, Philip would have slipped between the cracks of biblical history, and his name would have been lost forever. But in John's Gospel we find a brief, yet revealing, character sketch of Philip. We see him as scrutinizing, logical, somewhat pessimistic, and having a little difficulty stepping out in faith (see 1:43–46, 6:1–7, 12:20–22, 14:7–9).

> The next day He purposed to go forth into Galilee, and He found Philip. And Jesus said to him, "Follow Me." Now Philip was from Bethsaida, of the city of Andrew and Peter. (1:43–44)

Christ's approach with Philip was cold-contact evangelism. Apparently, they had never met before, and Jesus confronted him directly on the street. The message was "Follow Me." Simple and straightforward. No high-pressure sales pitch. No recruiting posters. No campaign promises. Just Jesus, calmly bidding "Follow Me." The response, although implied, was that Philip did follow Him.

D. Nathanael. Immediately and with serendipitous enthusiasm, Philip searched for Nathanael to tell him the good news.

> Philip found Nathanael and said to him, "We have found Him of whom Moses in the Law and also the Prophets wrote, Jesus of Nazareth, the son of Joseph." And Nathanael said to him, "Can any good thing come out of Nazareth?" Philip said to him, "Come and see." (vv. 45–46)

Keenly critical, Nathanael responds with unguarded candor—"Nazareth? You mean Sin City itself? Come on, Philip, get real." Yet his skepticism was honest; his brusqueness, without hypocrisy. And these were the very jewels Jesus saw sparkling beneath that lab coat of scientific skepticism.

> Jesus saw Nathanael coming to Him, and said of him, "Behold, an Israelite indeed, in whom is no guile!" (v. 47)[6]

---

6. The Hebrew word for *guile* originally referred to the bait used in catching fish. In time the word came to denote any cunning device or deceptive ploy. The Greek translation of the Old Testament uses *guile* in its description of Jacob when he deceived Isaac (Gen. 27:35). For further detail on this word, consult Leon Morris's *Reflections on the Gospel of John*, p. 63.

This perceptive greeting astonished Nathanael. He had never seen Jesus before and was quite sure that Jesus had never seen him.

Nathanael said to Him, "How do You know me?" Jesus answered and said to him, "Before Philip called you, when you were under the fig tree, I saw you." (v. 48)

Philip's approach to Nathanael resembles Andrew's approach to Peter. However, it is possible that the Word of God played an integral part in Nathanael's coming to Christ. The Jewish Talmud encouraged sincere, searching Jews to seek out places of solitude where they could pray, meditate, and study the Scriptures. Rabbinic writings give evidence that scholars and students often studied under shade trees. Perhaps Nathanael was digging into the Old Testament prophecies of the Messiah at the very time Jesus had seen him. That conjecture would certainly account for Nathanael's enthusiastic response when he met Christ.

Nathanael answered Him, "Rabbi, You are the Son of God; You are the King of Israel." Jesus answered and said to him, "Because I said to you that I saw you under the fig tree, do you believe? You shall see greater things than these." And He said to him, "Truly, truly, I say to you, you shall see the heavens opened, and the angels of God ascending and descending on the Son of Man." (vv. 49–51)

The message that formed a bridge from Nathanael's study of the Messiah to the person of Jesus was the words of Philip, "We have found Him of whom Moses in the Law and also the Prophets wrote, Jesus of Nazareth, the son of Joseph" (v. 45). The response was Nathanael's unqualified statement of faith (v. 49) and Jesus' promise that Nathanael would see great things as His disciple (vv. 50–51).

Echoes from the Old Testament

The entire Old Testament stands on tiptoe, anticipating the coming of the Messiah, God's anointed King of Israel (Pss. 2, 110).

In 1 Chronicles 28:9, David wisely counsels his son Solomon concerning his relationship with God: "If you seek Him, He will let you find Him."

Certainly this held true for Nathanael.

Certainly it can hold true for you as well.

📖 Living Insights

This passage deals specifically with the stories of five men who followed in faith. Let's take a closer look at the different evangelistic methods Christ used to win these men to Himself.

● Our study mentioned four approaches to evangelism: mass, personal, cold-contact, and the Word of God. Does one of these particularly interest you? See if you can discover additional New Testament accounts that show the same method in action. Or you may choose to look for another passage for each of the methods listed. A concordance would be helpful in this exercise. Record your findings and thoughts in the following charts.

Four Forms of Evangelism

Mass Evangelism	
Passages	Thoughts

Personal Evangelism	
Passages	Thoughts

Continued on next page

Cold-Contact Evangelism	
Passages	Thoughts

Evangelism Using the Word	
Passages	Thoughts

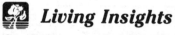 *Living Insights*

Study Two ▬▬▬▬▬▬▬▬▬▬▬▬▬▬▬▬▬▬▬▬▬▬▬▬▬▬▬▬▬▬▬▬

Before this study, were you aware of the different approaches to evangelism? Many people who have come to Christ through one style of evangelism are surprised to hear about other acceptable approaches. Often, the type of approach is more important to the presenter than to the listener.

- Use the following space to write down your thoughts about evangelism. Which approach appeals most to you? Is there a particular style that fits best with your personality? What keeps you from sharing the gospel with others, and what would help you begin to do it more? Be honest and write freely.

Evangelism and Me

_____

_____

_____

_____

_____

_____

_____

_____

_____

_____

_____

_____

_____

_____

Wine . . . Coins . . . and Signs
John 2

In 1980, wine buyers from all over the world gathered at the twelfth annual Heublein Rare Wine Auction in San Francisco. At the auction, a restaurant owner who had vowed to get "the finest bottle of wine in the world" spent $31,000 for a vintage 1822 bottle of Chateau Lafite Rothschild.

The well-heeled audience of more than three hundred wine connoisseurs gasped and applauded as the auctioneer slammed his gavel on the podium, ending the brisk, three-minute competition to capture this prized wine.[1] Valued not only for its rarity but also for its incomparable taste, Chateau Lafite continues to break auction records year after year.

But the world's finest wine was not made in the vineyards of France, nor was it served in the finest international restaurants. It was made and served at an unpretentious wedding in Cana of Galilee—two thousand years ago. And that wine is valued to this day, not for its rarity, but for what it reveals about its maker . . . Jesus Christ.

I. Outlining the Chapter
If you remember, the purpose of John's Gospel is to demonstrate that Jesus of Nazareth is the Son of God. In John 2, the author forcefully accomplishes this. But before we get into the individual verses, let's understand how this chapter fits within the framework of what has occurred before.

A. Chronologically. Chapter 2 begins with the words "And on the third day . . . " This raises the question: the third day of what? If you trace John's narrative in chapter 1, the chronology may become a little clearer. The first day of the account is found in 1:19; the second, 1:29; the third, 1:35; the fourth, 1:43. Therefore, the "third day" in 2:1 would be the third day after Philip's and Nathanael's conversions in 1:43–51.

B. Geographically. Mapped out in the first two chapters, Jesus' preaching itinerary takes Him to Bethany (1:28), Galilee (1:43), Cana of Galilee (2:1), Capernaum (2:12), and Jerusalem (2:13, 23).

C. Analytically. As we take a more analytical look at our passage, we find three incidents—involving wine, coins, and signs—each significant.

II. Understanding the Issues
The three incidents in John 2—wine at the wedding (vv. 1–11), coins in the temple (vv. 14–17), and signs for the Jews (vv. 18–22)—bring to light some very important issues.

---

1. "Memphis Man Spends $31,000 on 'Finest Wine,'" *Fort Worth Star-Telegram*, May 29, 1980.

A. Wine at the wedding. First-century weddings were considerably different than today's. A one-year betrothal period preceded the actual ceremony. Much more binding than modern-day engagements, only a bill of divorce could break it. According to the Mishnah—the second-century A.D. compilation of Jewish traditions—at the conclusion of the wedding ceremony, the groom and his guests made their way to the bride's home. This usually took place at night in a spectacular torchlight procession. There, speeches were made and expressions of goodwill publicly declared. Then everyone traveled to the groom's home, where a festive wedding banquet was held. This prolonged feast, mixing ceremony with celebration, lasted as long as a week. Hospitality was emphasized, and the hosts took great care to provide whatever the guests needed.[2]

1. The incident. The wedding feast, apparently large,[3] is recounted in verses 1–11.

> And on the third day there was a wedding in Cana of Galilee, and the mother of Jesus was there; and Jesus also was invited, and His disciples, to the wedding. And when the wine gave out, the mother of Jesus said to Him, "They have no wine." And Jesus said to her, "Woman, what do I have to do with you? My hour has not yet come." His mother said to the servants, "Whatever He says to you, do it." Now there were six stone waterpots set there for the Jewish custom of purification, containing twenty or thirty gallons each. Jesus said to them, "Fill the waterpots with water." And they filled them up to the brim. And He said to them, "Draw some out now, and take it to the headwaiter." And they took it to him. And when the headwaiter tasted the water which had become wine, and did not know where it came from (but the servants who had drawn the water knew), the headwaiter called the bridegroom, and said to him, "Every man serves the good wine first, and when men have drunk freely, then that which is poorer; you have kept the good wine until now." This beginning of His signs

2. For information on a typical Israelite marriage, consult *Ancient Israel: Social Institutions,* vol. 1, by Roland de Vaux (New York, N.Y.: McGraw-Hill Book Co., 1965), pp. 26–34.

3. Verse 6 notes six stone waterpots, containing 20 to 30 gallons each. Based on a 25-gallon average, the combined total would have been 150 gallons. At servings of 1 cup each, this would make 2,400 servings . . . and this was after the feast had been under way for some time.

Jesus did in Cana of Galilee, and manifested His glory, and His disciples believed in Him.

2. **The issue.** The real issue at the wedding was not the wine running out, but who replenished it. Jesus had taken ordinary water set aside to wash the guests' hands and eating utensils and used it to make the finest of wines (v. 10). The miracle was one of creation—a live demonstration that "all things came into being by Him" (1:3a). The miracle also demonstrated Jesus as Lord over time, since the wine, which normally needs much time to age, was fermented in only a fraction of a second. Thus was His glory revealed ... the veil of His earthly tabernacle raised, ever so briefly, ever so slightly, to let shine the Shekinah[4] that resided within (compare 2:11 with 1:14).

Water into Wine

With a touch, Jesus can take the murky water of our lives—so in need of purification—and transform it into fine wine.

Our lives need not sit tasteless, confined to stone waterpots on the sidelines of life. We can be full-bodied, free-flowing, and festive. All it takes is a little touch ... from a great and powerful God!

B. Coins in the temple. Verses 12–13 form a transition to the next incident in chapter 2.

After this He went down to Capernaum, He and His mother, and His brothers, and His disciples; and there they stayed a few days. And the Passover of the Jews was at hand, and Jesus went up to Jerusalem.

Passover—the greatest of all Jewish feasts.[5] By Jewish law, every male within fifteen miles of Jerusalem was required to make the journey to the sacred city for the celebration. And since every Jew dreamed of celebrating at least one Passover in Jerusalem, many more pilgrims came from outside that radius, swelling the city with as many as 2½ million visitors each year. Opportunistic Jewish officials put a sharp pencil to the situation and figured out how to make it a more rewarding stay—for themselves, that is, not for the travelers!

---

4. An Aramaic word meaning "resting place," the Shekinah glory referred to the visible symbol of God's presence in the tabernacle and afterward in Solomon's temple (Exod. 40:34–38, 1 Kings 8:10–13).

5. Passover is a time of remembrance for when God delivered Israel from Egypt (see Exod. 12).

1. **The incident.** When Jesus went to the temple courtyard, the scene infuriated Him.

> And He found in the temple those who were selling oxen and sheep and doves, and the money-changers seated. (v. 14)

Every Jew over nineteen was required to pay a temple tax, which could only be paid in Galilean or sanctuary shekels—hence, the need for moneychangers. The corruption, however, was not in the system but in the exorbitant rate these unscrupulous financiers charged. Adding to the corruption was the way sacrifices were approved. A fee was charged to inspect all animals brought to the temple for sacrifice. Most of the time, the inspectors found the animal blemished in some way, disqualifying it as a legitimate offering. This forced the out-of-town traveler to purchase an "approved" animal at the temple for often ten to twenty times the fair market value.[6] No wonder Christ was enraged.

> And He made a scourge of cords, and drove them all out of the temple, with the sheep and the oxen; and He poured out the coins of the money-changers, and overturned their tables; and to those who were selling the doves He said, "Take these things away; stop making My Father's house a house of merchandise." His disciples remembered that it was written, "Zeal for Thy house will consume me." (vv. 15–17)

2. **The issue.** This incident is clearly an account of removing from the temple those who were desecrating it. The issue is the sanctity of the temple, the dwelling place of deity. Today God dwells in the temple of our physical bodies (1 Cor. 6:19–20, 2 Cor. 5:1). The implications of this are enormous. We are not to allow the place where God dwells to become a house of merchandise—a loud, busy, deceptive place. It must be a place of prayer . . . a place of sanctity . . . a place of worship, where we can commune with God in spirit and in truth (John 4:23).

Cleansing the Temple

What do you allow to enter your "temple"? Does it enhance God's dwelling place—or does it defile and desecrate?

---

6. For a fuller discussion of the historical situation, consult *The Gospel of John,* vol. 1, rev. ed., by William Barclay (Edinburgh, Scotland: Saint Andrew Press, 1975), pp. 108–11.

> If the latter, expect a cleansing visit from Christ.
> And don't be surprised if a scourge accompanies Him
> (Heb. 12:5–11).

C. Signs for the Jews. The incident of Christ cleansing the temple brought Psalm 69:9 to the sensitive minds of the disciples. But the disgruntled merchandisers of faith—not so perceptive—wanted a little more positive identification. They wanted some authoritative sign (compare 1 Cor. 1:22).

1. **The incident.** Jesus not only overturned the moneychangers' business tables, He upended their mental tables as well.

   The Jews therefore answered and said to Him, "What sign do You show to us, seeing that You do these things?" Jesus answered and said to them, "Destroy this temple, and in three days I will raise it up." The Jews therefore said, "It took forty-six years to build this temple, and will You raise it up in three days?" But He was speaking of the temple of His body. When therefore He was raised from the dead, His disciples remembered that He said this; and they believed the Scripture, and the word which Jesus had spoken. (vv. 18–22)

2. **The issue.** The Jews wanted a sign; what they needed, however, was salvation. The issue was not what they *wanted to see;* it was what they *needed to believe.* This shallow type of faith, which substantiated itself on signs, prompted John to write the following postscript.

   Now when He was in Jerusalem at the Passover, during the feast, many believed in His name, beholding His signs which He was doing. But Jesus, on His part, was not entrusting Himself to them, for He knew all men, and because He did not need anyone to bear witness concerning man for He Himself knew what was in man. (vv. 23–25)

III. Applying the Truth

As we step back from these verses, our vision begins to adjust and we find that Christ is the focal point of each incident. In the wedding at Cana, John focuses on the glory of Christ. In the cleansing of the temple, he focuses on the liberating Christ. In the raising of the temple, on the indwelling Christ. We, too, need to focus on Jesus. In fact, that's our most desperate need—to become preoccupied with the Lord Jesus Christ. When at a gathering, if we're preoccupied with Christ, we won't be sidetracked by what's served, but we will

36

seek opportunities to share His glory. When rubbing shoulders with the world, if we're preoccupied with Christ, He will take charge and keep us clean. When living from one day to the next, if we're sufficiently preoccupied with Him, we won't need a lot of signs and wonders . . . just Christ.

 *Living Insights*

Study One ▬▬▬▬▬▬▬▬▬▬▬▬▬▬▬▬▬▬▬▬▬▬▬▬▬▬▬▬▬▬

What an exciting chapter! If television had existed in the first century, the wedding in Cana and the scene in the temple certainly would have made the nightly news. Let's take a closer look at these stories.

- A good way to get closer to a Scripture text is to write it out in your own words. Reread the twenty-five verses of John 2 and try your hand at paraphrasing the passage. Try to expand on the meanings of some of the key words and get in touch with the emotions felt by the characters.

My Paraphrase of John 2

_____

_____

_____

_____

_____

_____

_____

_____

_____

_____

_____

_____

_____

_____

Continued on next page

🌿 *Living Insights*

Wine at the wedding . . . coins in the temple . . . signs for the Jews— what does all this mean to you? Our study is rich in meaning for our lives, but we need to take the time and effort to apply it personally. Space is provided here for you to write how *you* can apply each section in this lesson. Be specific and realistic.

Wine at the Wedding

_____

_____

_____

_____

_____

_____

Coins in the Temple

_____

_____

_____

_____

_____

Signs for the Jews

_____

_____

_____

_____

_____

_____

Brainstorming the New Birth
John 3:1–21

July 2, 1505. Martin Luther, returning home from a visit with his parents, found himself caught in a violent storm. Terrified, he vowed to become a monk if he were allowed to live.

Luther made it through the storm and fulfilled his vow, entering the Augustinian order of monks in Erfurt, Germany. By his own admission, he entered the monastery more out of constraint than commitment. Reflecting on the incident years later, Luther said: "Not freely or desirously did I become a monk, but walled around with the terror and agony of sudden death, I vowed a constrained and necessary vow."[1]

While at the monastery and as a friar at the University of Wittenberg, Luther diligently, even obsessively, performed his religious tasks. He frequently went to confession and dutifully fulfilled the imposed penances.

But his hard work, his confessions, his penances never seemed enough. Anguished of soul, Luther wrestled with his own salvation. Hungering for acceptance by God, he realized his emptiness. Gnawing inside was the incessant, ravenous truth that his external righteousness wasn't enough: "For however irreproachably I lived as a monk, I felt myself in the presence of God to be a sinner with a most unquiet conscience, nor could I believe that I pleased him with my satisfactions."[2]

On a trip to Rome, which he thought would earn him some form of spiritual merit, he climbed the steps of Pilate's house on his knees. It is suggested by some church historians that this was where Luther first gained a true understanding of the gospel. As he climbed those stone-hard steps of religious works, a verse came to his mind that changed his life: Romans 1:17, "the righteous man shall live by faith." Like a flash of lightning, the realization struck him: It is *faith* that justifies—not works!

Luther looked back on that revelation as the time of his conversion: "At last I began to understand the justice of God as that by which the just man lives by the gift of God. . . . 'The just man shall live by faith.' At this I felt myself to have been born again, and to have entered through open gates into paradise itself."[3]

Luther had lived a rigorously religious life, pounding on heaven's door in the strength of his own works. Exhausted, he fell to his knees before that door and realized a liberating truth: Christ *Himself* is the door, and it

1. *Encyclopaedia Britannica,* 15th ed., see "Martin Luther."

2. *Encyclopaedia Britannica,* "Martin Luther."

3. *Encyclopaedia Britannica,* "Martin Luther."

opens to no human effort. Rather, the door swings on the well-oiled hinges of Christ's righteousness—and opens only by faith (John 10:9).

I. Contrast: Religion and Regeneration

Religion attempts to turn over new leaves; regeneration transforms lives. Religion is *man's effort to reach God*—our attempt to gain God's favor; regeneration is *God's effort to reach man*—His demonstration of love based on grace, aside from any merit on our part. Man's plan of salvation involves an external series of good works—church attendance, baptism, giving, benevolent deeds; God's plan is an internal gift from Himself—the impartation of new life by means of a spiritual rebirth. Luther spent years enmeshed in religious works, but it was not until he came to Christ by faith alone that he experienced regeneration.

II. Conversation: Nicodemus and Jesus

"Religious" people are often the most difficult to lead to Christ. They may be brilliant scholars, gifted leaders, or just "good folks," but they can suffer from a blindness that is almost impenetrable. A classic example is found in John 3.

A. Credentials (vv. 1, 10). Nicodemus had an impeccable resumé. If heaven could be earned from one's accomplishments, Nicodemus would have had change left over. In verses 1 and 10, we discover three salient facts about his background: he was "a man of the Pharisees[4] . . . a ruler of the Jews[5] . . . the teacher of Israel."[6]

B. Interchange (vv. 2–15). Undoubtedly, Nicodemus' credentials would have been severely undermined if he were seen with such a renegade as Jesus. Consequently, this renowned religious leader wrapped himself in the cloak of darkness to steal a few furtive moments with this controversial man—the one who changed water into wine and overturned tables in the temple. Perhaps, too, he saw evening as the best time for unhurried, undisturbed conversation. Little did Nicodemus realize, however, that when

4. The word *pharisee* comes from a Hebrew term that means "to be separated." Standing aloof from society in self-righteous smugness (compare Luke 18:9–14), the Pharisees were a tight-knit brotherhood dedicated to preserving, interpreting, and defending Jewish Law, which they legalistically forced upon the people of Israel. Commenting on the commandment to keep the Sabbath holy, these theological hair-splitters devoted sixty-four columns in the *Talmud* to Sabbath requirements. They also wrote twenty-four chapters in the *Mishnah* defining what qualified as work on the Sabbath and what didn't.

5. As ruler of the Jews, Nicodemus would have been a member of the Sanhedrin—a court of seventy men who had religious jurisdiction over every Jew in the world.

6. The fact that Jesus acknowledged Nicodemus as *the* teacher of Israel indicates that this religious leader had preeminent status in religious circles and was honored with an almost papal reverence.

he met with Jesus, he, the leading teacher of Israel, would be the one raising his hand and asking the elementary-school questions.
1. Theological discussion (vv. 2–13). Like a well-volleyed tennis match, an interchange of dialogue bounces back and forth between Nicodemus and Jesus.

This man came to Him by night, and said to Him, "Rabbi, we know that You have come from God as a teacher; for no one can do these signs that You do unless God is with him." (v. 2)

A high lob by Nicodemus, served politely into Jesus' court. But with a strong, precise shot, Jesus aims the conversation directly at the religious teacher's theological racket.

"Truly, truly, I say to you, unless one is born again, he cannot see the kingdom of God."[7] (v. 3)

Just as we must experience conception to begin physical, human life, so we must experience a rebirth, or conception from above, to begin spiritual, divine life (compare 1:12–13). But the metaphor catches Nicodemus off guard. Struggling to regain his balance, he backhands a question.

"How can a man be born when he is old? He cannot enter a second time into his mother's womb and be born, can he?" (v. 4)

Jesus positions Himself center court and answers,

"Truly, truly, I say to you, unless one is born of water[8] and the Spirit, he cannot enter into the kingdom of God. That which is born of the flesh is flesh, and that which is born of the Spirit is spirit. Do not marvel that I said to you, 'You must be born again.' The wind blows where it wishes and you hear the sound of it, but do not know where it comes from and where it is going; so is everyone who is born of the Spirit." (vv. 5–8)

Nicodemus reaches to return another question.

"How can these things be?" (v. 9)

---

7. The theme of the dialogue is the new birth. The term "born again," or *gennēthēi anōthen,* introduced here by Jesus, has never been used in the Bible up to this point. We get our word *regeneration* from the Latin rendering of the phrase "born again."

8. The phrase "born of water" is puzzling. Some commentators teach that it refers to baptism; others, to physical birth; others still, to the cleansing work of the Spirit when He comes into a person's life. Three reasons argue for the latter interpretation: (1) water was always used in certain pharisaic rites to symbolize cleansing; (2) because the original Greek uses only the one preposition *of* to govern two objects, neither having a definite article, the translation should read "of water (even) Spirit"; and (3) Titus 3:5 offers a parallel—"He saved us, not on the basis of deeds which we have done in righteousness, but according to His mercy, by the washing of regeneration and renewing by the Holy Spirit."

Jesus fires a power shot over the net, sending it squarely at Nicodemus's tightly strung heart.

"Are you the teacher of Israel, and do not understand these things? Truly, truly, I say to you, we speak that which we know, and bear witness of that which we have seen; and you do not receive our witness. If I told you earthly things and you do not believe, how shall you believe if I tell you heavenly things? And no one has ascended into heaven, but He who descended from heaven, even the Son of Man." (vv. 10–13)

2. **Historical illustration** (vv. 14–15). With a reference to Jewish history, Jesus brings the match to a close. Game: Jesus.

"And as Moses lifted up the serpent in the wilderness, even so must the Son of Man be lifted up; that whoever believes may in Him have eternal life."

A determined teacher, Jesus alludes to a familiar story in Numbers 21:4–9 in an effort to illustrate His point, which still seems hazy to Nicodemus. In the story, Israel was murmuring against the Lord so He sent fiery serpents among them as punishment. The serpents killed a number of people and made many others sick. As a remedy for their sin, God had Moses make a bronze serpent and raise it on a pole for all to see. If the people looked up at the serpent with even a hint of faith in God's provision, they were healed. All this was a striking foreshadow of Christ being lifted up on the cross to save those who were dying of sin and looked to Him in faith.

A Simple Look of Faith

The Israelites bitten by the serpents needed only to look with faith at God's provision for their sin to be healed.

They were not told to concoct some remedy. They were not told to fight the serpents . . . or make an offering . . . or pray . . . or even look to Moses.

All that was required was a simple look of faith. Like that of the thief on the cross, who merely looked to Jesus and said, "Remember me when You come into Your kingdom!" (Luke 23:42) . . . and the King answered, "Truly I say to you, today you shall be with Me in Paradise" (v. 43).

A simple look of faith—
That's all it took
To exchange a lifelong wilderness of shame
For paradise.

III. Clarification: Belief and Unbelief

At this point in the conversation, a footnote is added, the first verse of which has become the most quoted passage in all the Bible.

"For God so loved the world, that He gave His only begotten Son, that whoever believes in Him should not perish, but have eternal life. For God did not send the Son into the world to judge the world, but that the world should be saved through Him. He who believes in Him is not judged; he who does not believe has been judged already, because he has not believed in the name of the only begotten Son of God." (vv. 16–18)

This verbal match between Israel's top-seeded teachers clearly defines the issues. There are only two possible responses to Jesus: belief or unbelief. And there are only two possible destinies to which those responses lead: eternal life . . . or eternal death.

IV. Conclusion: Light and Darkness

Verses 19–21 are a theological postscript, explaining why some believe and others don't.

"And this is the judgment, that the light is come into the world, and men loved the darkness rather than the light; for their deeds were evil. For everyone who does evil hates the light, and does not come to the light, lest his deeds should be exposed. But he who practices the truth comes to the light, that his deeds may be manifested as having been wrought in God."

Ultimately, one's morality *does* influence one's theology. And sometimes to such an extent that many would rather skulk blindly in the dark cave of their sin, awaiting judgment, than bask, forgiven, in the dawn radiating from the true Light of this world.

A Happy Ending

Fortunately, like any good storyteller, John doesn't leave us in the dark regarding the outcome of the encounter between Nicodemus and Jesus. And it's a happy outcome to boot!

After Jesus was crucified, Joseph of Arimathea requested His body from Pilate so he could give his Savior a proper burial. Assisting in the burial was a man who now ventured to

---

> be seen with Jesus, fearless and unashamed, in the full light
> of day.
>   And Nicodemus came also, who had first come to
> Him by night; bringing a mixture of myrrh and aloes,
> about a hundred pounds weight. And so they took
> the body of Jesus, and bound it in linen wrappings
> with the spices, as is the burial custom of the Jews.
> (19:39–40)

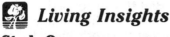 *Living Insights*

Study One

The historical backdrop to John 3:14–15 gives us much to ponder. Both historically and prophetically, the scene of Moses lifting up the serpent in the wilderness is significant. Let's compare the passage in Numbers with the account in John.

• Read Numbers 21:4–9 and picture the scene in your mind. What is the relationship between looking at that bronze image and believing in Jesus? Use the following chart to jot down points of similarity as you think through the comparison between the serpent and the Savior.

Numbers 21 and John 3—A Comparison	
Serpent in the Wilderness	Savior on the Cross

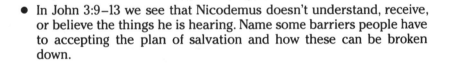

Living Insights

Let's devote this study to the "new birth." What does it really mean? Discuss your answers here on paper or with a group of friends.

- Read John 3:1–10. Put yourself in Nicodemus's place. Why was it so difficult for him to understand (note v. 10)? How can you present Christ to others in clear, simple terms? What is your favorite technique?

_____

_____

_____

_____

_____

_____

_____

_____

- In John 3:9–13 we see that Nicodemus doesn't understand, receive, or believe the things he is hearing. Name some barriers people have to accepting the plan of salvation and how these can be broken down.

_____

_____

_____

_____

_____

_____

_____

_____

Continued on next page

- Spend some time meditating on the most familiar verse in the Bible—John 3:16. Single out the verbs and see how they tell the truth of the gospel. Discuss the difference between salvation apart from works and salvation by works. Clarify what it means to believe. Finally, thank the Lord for His unconditional love for you.

_____

_____

_____

_____

_____

_____

_____

_____

_____

_____

_____

_____

The Preacher Who Lost His Congregation

John 3:22–36

"Truly, I say to you, among those born of women there has not arisen anyone greater than John the Baptist" (Matt. 11:11a).

That accolade from Jesus sounds like one that might have been conferred upon Moses, a man handpicked by God to deliver Israel from the Egyptians ... or upon David, who slew the giant and became the most renowned king in Israel's history ... or upon Daniel, the Winston Churchill of the Jews during their Babylonian captivity.

Instead, those laudatory words fell like garlands around the neck of an unsung hero named John. Unconventional, to say the least, John was an eccentric hermit living in the wilderness, proclaiming an uncompromising message of repentance to prepare the people's hearts for the Messiah.

Clothed in camel hair and a leather belt, he was hardly dressed for success. His Spartan diet of locusts and honey would never have sparked a culinary trend, even among the most austere of nutritionists. And with his abrasive rhetoric, John wouldn't have been a likely choice for any political hopeful's campaign manager.

Yet Jesus picked this enigma of a man to represent Him as His forerunner, a job with three primary functions: *to clear the way*—to remove obstacles from the minds and hearts of others so they would be ready for the Messiah; *to prepare the way*—to promote repentance on the part of the nation so He would be accepted; and *to get out of the way*—to step aside once the Messiah had been introduced.

In this lesson, we'll see him getting out of the way ... probably the toughest part of his job description and, undoubtedly, the reason Jesus called him a great man.

I. Biographical Situation: He Must Increase

Like a small lamp held high in some obscure corner of a dark house, John upheld a solitary wick of testimony about Jesus, the true light of the world. But as others began to follow him, John became well aware that his ministry and Jesus' had all the potential for competition. But because the wick was content to serve the Light, any shadows of conflict were quickly dispelled. Watch how a potentially volatile situation arises—and how John humbly handles it.

A. Location of Jesus and John. To begin with, notice that their two ministries were operating on the same turf (compare 3:22 with Matt. 3:1).

47

After these things Jesus and His disciples came into the land of Judea, and there He was spending time with them and baptizing.[1] And John also was baptizing in Aenon near Salim, because there was much water there; and they were coming and were being baptized. For John had not yet been thrown into prison. (John 3:22–24)

Jesus' ministry had been in Galilee up to this time. Now He moves into John's domain. Territorial creatures that we are, mere geographical proximity could have created conflict, as it did between the herdsmen of Abram and Lot (Gen. 13:1–12). In fact, although John wasn't bothered, a little friction from his disciples does begin to heat up the Judean wilderness.

B. Discussion among John's disciples. A man in John's audience, a Jew who had probably heard Jesus' teaching, sparks a debate with a question about ceremonial washing.

There arose therefore a discussion on the part of John's disciples with a Jew about purification. (v. 25)

The Greek word for *discussion* is the term from which we get our word *diatribe*, meaning "a prolonged discourse; a bitter and abusive speech." Because of this verbal confrontation, apparently rooted in Jesus' teaching, John's disciples come to him, complaining that he is losing some of his flock to this fledgling preacher.

And they came to John and said to him, "Rabbi, He who was with you beyond the Jordan, to whom you have borne witness, behold, He is baptizing, and all are coming to Him." (v. 26)

"Hey Preacher, you gotta do something! Attendance is way down, and we're losing a lot of members to that new church down the street!" Sound familiar? John's disciples are feeling the crunch of competition. But instead of inventing some glitzy gimmick to recapture the thinning multitudes, John pulls a different strategy out of his camel hair sleeve.

C. Reaction of the forerunner. John's response throws cold water on his inflamed disciples, quenching the conversation and their competitive spirit.

"A man can receive nothing, unless it has been given him from heaven. You yourselves bear me witness,

---

1. The verb phrase "spending time" comes from a term meaning "to rub hard" or "rub through." The idea is one of rubbing shoulders with others long enough to get into their lives. The imperfect tense of the verbs in the phrase "was spending time with them and baptizing" indicates that Jesus kept doing this or continued to do so (the same tense is used of John baptizing in v. 23).

that I said, 'I am not the Christ,' but, 'I have been sent before Him.' He who has the bride is the bridegroom; but the friend of the bridegroom, who stands and hears him, rejoices greatly because of the bridegroom's voice. And so this joy of mine has been made full. He must increase, but I must decrease." (vv. 27–30) His response incorporates four ideas. First, God is in charge—not man (v. 27). Second, all work is significant—but only one work is preeminent (v. 28). Third, joy comes from being obedient, not from getting glory (v. 29). Fourth, humility calls attention to Christ, not self (v. 30). A similar response can be seen in Moses as he deals with the competitive spirit that has surfaced in his followers regarding two young, upstart prophets.

But two men had remained in the camp; the name of one was Eldad and the name of the other Medad. And the Spirit rested upon them (now they were among those who had been registered, but had not gone out to the tent), and they prophesied in the camp. So a young man ran and told Moses and said, "Eldad and Medad are prophesying in the camp." Then Joshua the son of Nun, the attendant of Moses from his youth, answered and said, "Moses, my lord, restrain them." But Moses said to him, "Are you jealous for my sake? Would that all the Lord's people were prophets, that the Lord would put His Spirit upon them!" (Num. 11:26–29)

Coping with Envy and Jealousy

"Jealously and envy are often used interchangeably, but there is a difference. Envy begins with empty hands, mourning for what it *doesn't* have. . . . Jealousy is not quite the same. It begins with full hands but is threatened by the loss of its plenty. It is the pain of losing what I have to someone else."[2]

John and Moses certainly knew how to cope with envy and jealousy. So did the psalmist who wrote:

For not from the east, nor from the west,
Nor from the desert comes exaltation;
But God is the Judge;
He puts down one, and exalts another.
(Ps. 75:6–7)

2. Charles R. Swindoll, *Killing Giants, Pulling Thorns* (Portland, Oreg.: Multnomah Press, 1978), p. 23.

Envy often rears its ugly head when one of your peers is promoted ... when a newcomer passes you on the way up the corporate ladder ... when you're a senior on the bench and a sophomore is in the starting line-up ... when a new business sprouts up and overshadows yours overnight.

Envy's evil twin, jealousy, tags along when loyalties shift ... when close friends abandon us for others ... when retirement comes and our authority is handed to a replacement.

Like seedy muggers in a dark alley, envy and jealousy wait to do us in—to rob us of our joy, work us over, and leave our spiritual lives for dead.

Are you going to let that happen to you? The only way to stop it is to walk down another street, the well-lit street of humility—a street illumined not by our own light but by the light of another, whose sandal we are not worthy to untie.

II. Doctrinal Declaration

In John 3:31–35, our humble forerunner delivers his doctrinal statement on the person of Christ, progressively unfurling a leaf of truth that stems from the prologue in chapter 1.

"He who comes from above is above all, he who is of the earth is from the earth and speaks of the earth. He who comes from heaven is above all. What He has seen and heard, of that He bears witness; and no man receives His witness. He who has received His witness has set his seal to this, that God is true. For He whom God has sent speaks the words of God; for He gives the Spirit without measure. The Father loves the Son, and has given all things into His hand."

At the end of his message, John gives an altar call that would jostle even the most complacent off the fence!

"He who believes in the Son has eternal life; but he who does not obey the Son shall not see life, but the wrath of God abides on him." (v. 36)

Moment of Decision

In verse 29, John refers to himself as "the friend of the bridegroom," a rough equivalent to our culture's best man.

According to Jewish tradition, the friend was a liaison between the bride and the bridegroom. He would arrange the details of the wedding—such as sending out invitations, making announcements, and presiding over the marriage feast. His special duty, however, was to guard the bridal chamber.

He would let no one into that chamber except the bride, who secretly slipped away from the celebrating crowd to join the groom. Sometime later, after the union was consummated, the groom came out and announced the fact with a shout. Upon hearing the groom's voice, the friend of the bridegroom would be happy and relieved. His job was done. His joy was full. He could now step out of the way.

John is saying, essentially, "I'm like the friend. I do my task best when I've stepped out of the way."

How about you? Are you content to be the faceless, offstage voice announcing the star of the show? Can you give Jesus center stage while you operate the curtains and unveil Him to the audience? Can you turn the spotlight away from yourself and onto Him?

You can if you become a person like John . . . if you're willing to play a minor part without upstaging the lead and stealing the show yourself.

That will be easy if Jesus is truly *first* in your life. And you can tell whether He is first if you're happy in *second* place, and if you're willing to surrender *any* spotlight to Him.

 Living Insights

Study One ▬▬▬▬▬▬▬▬▬▬▬▬▬▬▬▬▬▬▬▬▬▬▬▬▬▬▬▬▬▬

The more you study John the Baptizer, the more you have to respect him. In the passage we've just studied, we see the last mention of him in the apostle's Gospel. Do you know how the life of John the Baptizer ended? Let's find out.

- Accounts of John's death are found in Matthew 14:1–12 and Mark 6:14–29. Read them and summarize the story in the space provided.

The Death of John the Baptizer

_____

_____

_____

_____

Continued on next page

_____

_____

_____

_____

_____

_____

_____

_____

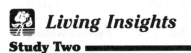 *Living Insights*

Study Two ▬▬▬▬▬▬▬▬▬▬▬▬▬▬▬▬▬▬▬▬▬▬▬▬▬▬

The application of John the Baptizer's teaching centers on the pre-eminence of Christ...giving Him first place in your life. What does that mean for you? Have you given Him first place? If so, how has your life changed since then? Was it a one-time decision, or is it a daily one? What are your biggest struggles in releasing areas of control? Jot down your thoughts in the space provided.

Giving God First Place in My Life

_____

_____

_____

_____

_____

_____

_____

_____

Water for a Thirsty Woman
John 4:1–42

Jesus offered living water to a sun-parched woman at a Samaritan well—water that all humanity thirsts for. Professor Zane Hodges discusses this longing in his excellent book, *The Hungry Inherit.*

> Love, success, wealth, fame—these were but a few of the countless springs at which men had stooped to drink, only to rise from them to find that they offered no lasting inward satisfaction, no enduring personal fulfillment....
>
> But His water was different! It could accomplish a miracle! The one who drank it was secure from thirst, not merely for time but for eternity as well.... So vital, so transforming was such a drink, that in the innermost being of the man who drank it, there was created an inexhaustible fountain of life. The waters of that hidden inner spring could not run dry; they could not be stanched; they virtually leaped up to produce the surpassing experience of eternal life.[1]

Such was the experience of the Samaritan woman in John 4, and such is the offer to all who come to Christ. With one sip of faith, our deepest thirst is quenched. And what was once a wilderness of wants is transformed into an oasis overflowing with abundant life.

Journeying back through the years of time, let's stop now and rest at the well where that offer was first made.

I. The Setting
In verses 1–2, we find the Pharisees getting wind of Jesus' rising popularity. When Jesus realizes this, He takes His disciples and leaves Judea for Galilee (v. 3). En route, He passes through Samaria (v. 4). Exhausted by the long trip, He comes to rest at a well outside the town of Sychar—Jacob's well, to be exact (vv. 5–6). It is the sixth hour of the day, just about noon, and the impartial Palestinian sun beats down on this tired traveler. His hungry disciples, meanwhile, have gone ahead into the city for food. As His weary, waiting eyes scan the horizon, His unsuspecting appointment arrives, carrying a waterpot on her head.

II. The Conversation
In those days, women normally drew water at dawn or dusk, the cooler hours of the day. It was a time to visit, to exchange news, to idle away a little time gossiping. That this woman has come to the well at noon, the hottest hour of the day, hints at her reputation

---

1. Zane Clark Hodges, *The Hungry Inherit* (Chicago, Ill.: Moody Press, 1972), pp. 13–14.

(compare vv. 18 and 28). Promiscuous with the men and, consequently, cold-shouldered by the women, she braves the brazen sun to avoid the searing stares of the more reputable.

A. The discussion (vv. 7–26). The woman comes bearing a dry, empty pot, a telling symbol of her parched, barren heart. Jesus opens the conversation with a direct, and somewhat disarming, request.

"Give Me a drink." (v. 7)

But she responds defensively to His simple petition (v. 9).

"How is it that You, being a Jew, ask me for a drink since I am a Samaritan woman?" (For Jews have no dealings with Samaritans.)

Intense racial hatred existed between Jews and Samaritans, much of it centering on religious differences.[2] So great was this animosity that, in traveling from Judea to Galilee, Jews would go miles out of their way to avoid crossing the Samaritan border.[3] And not only is our noonday patron of the well a Samaritan—she is a woman. Cultural sentiment for women was extremely low during the time of Christ. The Pharisees taught that men should not speak to women in public.[4] Some men were even so rigid as to refuse to look at a woman they passed on the street. But Christ not only looks at her and speaks with her, He does so kindly and in such a way as to whet her appetite for spiritual things.

Jesus answered and said to her, "If you knew the gift of God, and who it is who says to you, 'Give Me a drink,' you would have asked Him, and He would have given you living water." (v. 10)

But His alluring conversation is met with skepticism and sarcasm.

She said to Him, "Sir, You have nothing to draw with and the well is deep; where then do You get that living water? You are not greater than our father

---

2. For example, the Samaritans had as their Scripture the five books of Moses—Genesis through Deuteronomy. The Jews, having the entire Old Testament as their Scripture, looked down on the religion of the Samaritans as impoverished and incomplete. For more information on the rift between the Jews and Samaritans, consult Leon Morris's *The Word Was Made Flesh: John 1–5*, vol. 1 of *Reflections on the Gospel of John* (Grand Rapids, Mich.: Baker Book House, 1986), pp. 120–23.

3. For strict Jews, the route for travel from Jerusalem to Galilee lay through the region beyond the Jordan. The shortcut through Samaria was used only by those in a hurry.

4. Leon Morris quotes the rabbinic attitude toward women at the time of Christ: "He that talks much with womankind brings evil upon himself." One of the Jewish prayers included the phrase, "Blessed are thou, O Lord . . . who has not made me a woman." *The Gospel According to John*, from *The New International Commentary on the New Testament*, ed. F. F. Bruce (Grand Rapids, Mich.: William B. Eerdmans Publishing Co., 1971), p. 274, n. 68.

Jacob, are You, who gave us the well, and drank of it
himself, and his sons, and his cattle?" (vv. 11–12)
With her who-do-you-think-you-are question, the woman makes
a mild attempt at putting Jesus in His place. But Jesus responds
by patiently appealing to her immediate desire for physical
water. And, in doing so, He appeals to her greater, though less
obvious, spiritual thirst.

Jesus answered and said to her, "Everyone who drinks
of this water shall thirst again; but whoever drinks
of the water that I shall give him shall never thirst;
but the water that I shall give him shall become in
him a well of water springing up to eternal life."
(vv. 13–14)

However, seeing only from a human viewpoint, the woman misses
His point entirely.

The woman said to Him, "Sir, give me this water, so
I will not be thirsty, nor come all the way here to
draw." (v. 15)

Feeling that the conversation is beginning to meander down a
dead-end path, Jesus points to her personal life. In effect, He
places a full-length mirror in front of her, forcing her to take a
good, hard look at herself.

He said to her, "Go, call your husband, and come
here." (v. 16)

Like the sobering reflection that greets you when you first wake
up, this woman's glimpse of herself makes her flush with embarrassment. But when she tries to skirt the mirrored issues, Jesus
nudges her into facing the emptiness within her heart.

The woman answered and said, "I have no husband."
Jesus said to her, "You have well said, 'I have no
husband'; for you have had five husbands, and the
one whom you now have is not your husband; this
you have said truly." (vv. 17–18)

Christ's sharp perception pricks her conscience, and the desola-
tion and shame is more than she can bear. Squirming, she shifts
to more comfortable conversation.

"Sir, I perceive that You are a prophet. Our fathers
worshiped in this mountain, and you people say that
in Jerusalem is the place where men ought to worship." (vv. 19–20)

What about the heathen in Africa? How can a good God allow
suffering and evil? What about creation and evolution? Sprin-
kling or immersion . . . wine or grape juice . . . King James or Living Bible? Distracting questions about religious peripherals. This

is the smoke screen she hopes will hide her blemished soul from the dawning light of His penetrating gaze. But it is no use. A radiant shaft of truth pierces the veil.

> Jesus said to her, "Woman, believe Me, an hour is coming when neither in this mountain, nor in Jerusalem, shall you worship the Father. You worship that which you do not know; we worship that which we know, for salvation is from the Jews. But an hour is coming, and now is, when the true worshipers shall worship the Father in spirit and truth; for such people the Father seeks to be His worshipers. God is spirit, and those who worship Him must worship in spirit and truth." (vv. 21–24)

He clears away the mist: it is not *where* one worships that matters; it is *how* and, ultimately, *who* one worships that is important. Jesus brings the conversation to such a burning focus that her very soul is on the verge of igniting.

> The woman said to Him, "I know that Messiah is coming (He who is called Christ); when that One comes, He will declare all things to us." (v. 25)

B. The declaration (v. 26). A foreigner, a Samaritan, a woman, and, to top it all off, a woman of low morals and ill repute. To a strict Jew, she is indeed far from the kingdom of God. But because of a man she knows simply as "a Jew" (v. 9) . . . then as "Sir" (v. 15) . . . then as "a prophet" (v. 19), she now crouches on the brink of total acceptance, waiting to make that leap of faith—somewhat fearfully, but most certainly—as her ears listen with piqued interest for the revealing of this mysterious visitor's true identity.

> Jesus said to her, "I who speak to you am He." (v. 26)

III. The Reaction

Just at that dramatic, cliff-hanging moment, guess who shows up with the burgers and fries? The disciples. It's an awkward situation for everyone—everyone, that is, except Jesus.

> And at this point His disciples came, and they marveled that He had been speaking with a woman; yet no one said, "What do You seek?" or, "Why do You speak with her?" (v. 27)

A. Of the Samaritan woman.

> So the woman left her waterpot, and went into the city, and said to the men, "Come, see a man who told me all the things that I have done; this is not the Christ, is it?" (vv. 28–29)

The Moment of Faith

"Like the sun bursting forth from behind the clouds, the light of truth had flooded her soul. She turned from Him, the waterjar she had come to fill standing empty upon the ground, but the heart she had not come to fill now overflowing with living water."[5]

Just as Jesus had earlier turned tepid water into the most festive of wines, He now takes the emptiest of lives and fills it full.

He can do that with your life too. No matter how stagnant the water...no matter how empty the pot.

All it takes is a sip of faith.

B. Of the Samaritan men. Like a stone plopped into water, Jesus' words of life fall into the Samaritan woman's heart and then ripple through the city. The response to this one changed life is overwhelming. Swells of people flow from the city and pour over the countryside on their way to Jesus.

They went out of the city, and were coming to Him.... And from that city many of the Samaritans believed in Him because of the word of the woman who testified, "He told me all the things that I have done." So when the Samaritans came to Him, they were asking Him to stay with them; and He stayed there two days. And many more believed because of His word; and they were saying to the woman, "It is no longer because of what you said that we believe, for we have heard for ourselves and know that this One is indeed the Savior of the world." (vv. 30, 39–42)

A solitary seed has been planted, and within the time it takes to eat lunch, an entire field of humanity becomes ripe for harvest for the kingdom of God.

C. Of the disciples. Meanwhile, the disciples have their minds on a more pressing matter—food!

The disciples were requesting Him, saying, "Rabbi, eat." But He said to them, "I have food to eat that you do not know about." The disciples therefore were saying to one another, "No one brought Him anything to eat, did he?" (vv. 31–33)

But while they're preoccupied with passing the salt and catsup, Jesus teaches them a vital lesson about another kind of food.

---

5. Hodges, *The Hungry Inherit,* p. 18.

"My food is to do the will of Him who sent Me, and to accomplish His work. Do you not say, 'There are yet four months, and then comes the harvest'? Behold, I say to you, lift up your eyes, and look on the fields, that they are white for harvest. Already he who reaps is receiving wages, and is gathering fruit for life eternal; that he who sows and he who reaps may rejoice together. For in this case the saying is true, 'One sows, and another reaps.' I sent you to reap that for which you have not labored; others have labored, and you have entered into their labor." (vv. 34–38)

A Concluding Application

The Samaritan woman needed water. But the disciples, whose thirst had already been quenched by the river of life, needed food.

A sinner's greatest need is the free gift of salvation. The greatest need of one who is saved is to understand and do the will of God.

For you who are empty and don't know Jesus personally, like the Samaritan woman—you are offered the incredible gift of eternal life. For you whom Jesus has already brought into His family, like the disciples—you are given the incomparable offer to work with Him side by side, receiving the laborer's reward and sharing in the joy of the harvest.

What an incredible and incomparable Savior, who not only gives us the grace to receive Him but also the dignity of serving with Him in ripened fields (Eph. 2:8–10).

Living Insights

Study One

In the prejudiced society of first-century Palestine, there was no lower person in the system than a Samaritan woman—especially one with loose morals. Yet John 4 records a wonderful encounter between such a person and her Savior.

• One of the keys to good inductive Bible study is the ability to ask questions of the text. Learning to do that requires observation. Examine the story in John 4. Ask questions as you read, and record your questions in the space provided. As a suggestion, try the typical investigative questions—*who, what, where, when, why,* and *how.* Find the answers within the passage itself.

John 4:1–42

Question: _____

_____

Answer: _____

_____

Question: _____

_____

Answer: _____

_____

Question: _____

_____

Answer: _____

_____

Question: _____

_____

Answer: _____

_____

Question: _____

_____

Answer: _____

_____

Question: _____

_____

Answer: _____

_____

Continued on next page

📖 Living Insights

It would have been very easy for Jesus to pass right by the woman at the well. Most would have considered her unimportant, unlovely, insignificant. But Jesus didn't... He took the time to show her what was really important in life. How do you rate in the matter of loving the unlovely?

- How do you feel about those less fortunate than you? Do you reach out to minister to them, or are they conveniently overlooked in your day-to-day life? Take a few minutes to answer the following questions.

1. Who in my life is less fortunate than I?

_____

_____

_____

2. What are some specific ways I could minister to this person?

_____

_____

_____

_____

_____

3. How can I build this ministry into my everyday life?

_____

_____

_____

_____

_____

Healing at a Distance

John 4:46–54

Most Americans can expect to live about seventy years, according to statistics. But the statistical tables don't always work out with real-life precision. For example, we expect to face the deaths of our parents someday. We don't expect, however, to face the deaths of our children.

Neither did Nicholas Wolterstorff.

But one bright Sunday afternoon, a numbing telephone call brought news of a mountain-climbing accident. In his book *Lament for a Son,* the bereaved father reflects upon his painful feelings.

> Gone from the face of the earth. I wait for a group of students to cross the street, and suddenly I think: He is not there. I go to a ballgame and find myself singling out the twenty-five-year olds; none of them is he. In all the crowds and streets and rooms and churches and schools and libraries and gatherings of friends in our world, on all the mountains, I will not find him. Only his absence.
>
> Silence. "Was there a letter from Eric today?" "When did Eric say he would call?" Now only silence. Absence and silence.
>
> When we gather now there's always someone missing, his absence as present as our presence, his silence as loud as our speech. Still five children, but one always gone.
>
> When we're all together, we're not all together.
>
> It's the *neverness* that is so painful. *Never again* to be here with us—never to sit with us at table, never to travel with us, never to laugh with us, never to cry with us, never to embrace us as he leaves for school, never to see his brothers and sister marry. All the rest of our lives we must live without him.[1]

As we turn to our lesson in John 4, the emotion of another father who fears the death of his son bleeds through the page.

I. The Occasion

The first miracle Jesus performed was the turning of water into wine at the wedding feast in Cana (2:11). In chapter 4, verses 46–54, John records a second miracle—the healing of a government official's son who lay sick some twenty miles away. Two major characters enact this emotionally charged drama: Jesus and the royal official. The word translated "royal official" is *basilikos,* meaning "king's man." Obviously a person of prestigious rank, this man is probably one of

1. Nicholas Wolterstorff, *Lament for a Son* (Grand Rapids, Mich.: William B. Eerdmans Publishing Co., 1987), pp. 14–15.

61

Herod's trusted officers. But his rank means nothing to him now. His son's life is at stake. Consequently, he doesn't go to Herod; he goes to Jesus, the very source of life. Amazing, isn't it, how infirmity draws people to Christ faster than prosperity does. But sometimes that's what it takes. As C. S. Lewis observed: "how hard it is to turn our thoughts to God when everything is going well with us."[2]

II. The Conversation

Cupping our ears to overhear the conversation between the royal official and Jesus, we can't help but empathize with this troubled father.

> There was a certain royal official, whose son was sick at Capernaum. When he heard that Jesus had come out of Judea into Galilee, he went to Him, and was requesting Him to come down and heal his son; for he was at the point of death. (vv. 46b–47)

The imperfect tense of the verb *requesting* gives the nuance of continuous action. It could be paraphrased "he kept on begging Him over and over again." Like so many of Christ's followers, the official thought Jesus had to be right by his son's bedside to effectively handle the situation. Although we can understand his urgency, we shouldn't overlook two matters: (1) he told Christ how to handle the need, and (2) he presented the need before presenting himself. How much better it would have been for him to simply lay himself and his problem at the feet of Christ and allow Jesus to handle it *His* way. As we listen to Jesus' response, we might feel, at first glance, that He comes down awfully hard on this desperate father.

> Jesus therefore said to him, "Unless you people see signs and wonders, you simply will not believe." (v. 48)

Before we judge Jesus' words too harshly, we must understand that a "circus" atmosphere was developing around Christ. To many people, He was fast becoming a traveling sideshow—"Come one, come all! See the Galilean Miracle Worker!" No doubt tearful by now, the broken father persisted. And the persistence of this royal official won him a hearing before the true King.

> The royal official said to Him, "Sir, come down before my child dies." Jesus said to him, "Go your way; your son lives." The man believed the word that Jesus spoke to him, and he started off. (vv. 49–50)

But why didn't Jesus go to Capernaum Himself? Probably, He wanted to stretch the faith of this official. Standing by and watching as another brings healing requires little faith. But to believe without being there, without seeing for yourself—that takes faith!

---

2. C. S. Lewis, *The Problem of Pain* (New York, N.Y.: The Macmillan Co., 1962), p. 96.

Time to Smell the Flowers

We tend to envision long, full lives for all of our children. We forget, though, that the first grave dug was for a son, not a father (Gen. 4:1–11).

Like a blooming orchard caught in an untimely frost, the fruit of the womb is sometimes nipped coldly in the bud.

If you have a blossoming family, now is the time to treasure its fragrance—every unique flower, each individual petal—for you never know if the weather might turn suddenly cold.

III. The Reaction

A. The official: belief. The royal official followed Jesus' instructions to be on his way. At first glance, we might assume that he was hurrying back to Capernaum. But the Greek verb for "started off"—*poreuō*—simply means "to go one's way." All we can infer is that he left Jesus' presence absolutely assured that His words formed a promise. And in that promise, he rested. Most likely, he stayed in Cana and went about the business he was there for. Verses 51–52 support that speculation.

> And as he was now going down, his slaves met him, saying that his son was living. So he inquired of them the hour when he began to get better. They said therefore to him, "Yesterday at the seventh hour the fever left him."

Remember now, the towns were no more than twenty miles apart—for a man in a hurry, no more than a four- to five-hour walk. If the healing took place at the seventh hour of the day, or 1:00 P.M., the official could have been home well before nightfall. But note how his servants greet him on the road: "Yesterday . . ." The man must have placed such confidence in Jesus' promise that he didn't return home until the next day. That's faith!

B. The slaves: excitement. The imperfect tense of the verb *saying* in verse 51 indicates continual action. Apparently, the slaves were jumping up and down with joy, repeating over and over: "Your son's alive . . . he's living . . . he's well!"

C. The household: revival. The healing not only caused enthusiasm on the road, it created a revival at home.

> So the father knew that it was at that hour in which Jesus said to him, "Your son lives"; and he himself believed, and his whole household. (v. 53)

An interesting cross-reference to this verse is found in Luke 8:1–3.

And it came about soon afterwards, that He began going about from one city and village to another, proclaiming and preaching the kingdom of God; and the twelve were with Him, and also some women who had been healed of evil spirits and sicknesses: Mary who was called Magdalene, from whom seven demons had gone out, and Joanna the wife of Chuza, Herod's steward, and Susanna, and many others who were contributing to their support out of their private means.

Look closely at verse 3. Joanna was the wife of Chuza, Herod's steward, who was in charge of the king's financial books—a close, trusted official, occasionally called "the king's man." Yet, though the king's man, he and his wife supported Jesus out of their private means. Very possibly, Chuza and Joanna were the grateful parents of the young man healed in John 4.

IV. Conclusion

John concludes the story of the royal official's son with an editorial comment found in verse 54.

This is again a second sign that Jesus performed, when He had come out of Judea into Galilee.

This statement directly ties in with John's major purpose in writing the book, that the reader might "believe that Jesus is the Christ" (20:31).

V. Application

This moving account of Christ's compassion dramatically illustrates His lordship, not only over the physical realm with regard to sickness, but over the spatial realm as well, as His power to heal spanned a distance of twenty miles. Those of us who are fathers can learn a great deal from this account.

A. A faithful father isn't too independent to admit his needs (vv. 46–49). This father sought help when faced with a critical situation. He wasn't afraid to admit his own inadequacy or to ask for help publicly. He didn't pretend to be a stoic pillar of independent strength. How vulnerable are you? How honest are you about your needs . . . with yourself? With God? With your wife? With others?

B. A faithful father isn't too busy to know his children. This father didn't send his wife—"Honey, you take care of it; I've got a lot of work stacked up at the royal office." He went himself. He was involved in his home. Men, do you delegate too much family responsibility to your wife? If you do, she may find it hard to believe you really care.

C. A faithful father isn't too proud to believe God's Word
(vv. 50, 53). Maybe, at this very moment, you are separated by
distance from a situation you are concerned about. Will you
trust God to be there? Will you take Him at His Word? Maybe
God has you waiting . . . flat on your back or away from home . . .
forcing you to believe Him.

D. A faithful father isn't too logical to walk by faith. Are
you a pacesetter in spiritual things? When the members of your
family need counsel, do they turn to you? Do you promote
Christian activities or are you a barrier to them? If God were to
take you this afternoon, would your joyful, free life of faith be
what your family remembers most about you?

**E. A faithful father isn't too serious to enjoy life with
his family.** A painful moment of honesty, please. Is this you?
"You kids shut up! . . . Turn out those lights. . . . Get that room
cleaned up. . . . It costs too much. You think money grows on
trees?" God didn't create you to be a sergeant, or the home to
be a boot camp, or your children to be Marine Corps recruits.
He gave you a family to nurture . . . as a gardener nurtures his
plants.

> How blessed is everyone who fears the Lord,
> Who walks in His ways.
> When you shall eat of the fruit of your hands,
> You will be happy and it will be well with you.
> Your wife shall be like a fruitful vine,
> Within your house,
> Your children like olive plants
> Around your table.
> Behold, for thus shall the man be blessed
> Who fears the Lord. (Ps. 128:1–4)

And God gave you a family not only to nurture but to enjoy as
well. Will your children remember their childhood as being fun . . .
or frantic? The world outside your front door is cold enough.
But when the fire flickers out at home . . . how great is the darkness, how piercing the cold.

Living Insights

Study One

Distance is no barrier to God! Location has nothing to do with His
healing. God works effectively no matter where the sick or afflicted
may be. This powerful portion of Scripture deserves a closer look.

Continued on next page

- Action fills this passage. Using the chart that follows, record all the verbs in the left column. In the center column, jot down the verse where each verb appears. Finally, in the right column, give the meanings of these action words.

John 4:46–54 . . . A Passage of Action		
Verbs	Verses	Meanings

📖 Living Insights

Our study ended with some great application-oriented truths for those of us who are parents. Are you a parent best described by the word *faithful?* What pointers did you pick up from the lesson that you can apply in your relationships with your family? Think through these questions and use the following space to record your answers.

Becoming a Faithful Parent

_____

_____

_____

_____

_____

_____

_____

_____

_____

_____

_____

_____

_____

_____

_____

_____

_____

An Exposé of Legalism
John 5:1–18

"Thou shalt."
"Thou shalt not."
"Thou shalt!"
"Shalt not!"
"Shalt!"
"Not!"
"SHALT!"
"NOT!"

Sounds like angry children arguing on the playground, doesn't it? But what you're hearing is the insistent bickering of adult Christians entrenched in legalism.

Legalists measure spiritual growth against a yardstick notched incrementally by good works. Like rigid, unrelenting grade-school teachers, they rap their students' knuckles when they don't measure up.

Self-made standards. They may conveniently size people up, but in the end, they stunt growth instead of measure it.

The Pharisees are the grandfathers of legalism, and in our Scripture passage today, Jesus meets them in a head-to-head, toe-to-toe confrontation that turns the tide of official opinion against Him.

I. Legalism—Let's Understand It
When we lift the veil on legalism, we find hypocrisy instead of holiness. Let's take a closer look and expose it for the whitewashed tomb it is.

A. What is it? Legalism is conforming to a code of behavior for the purpose of exalting self. Legalists make lists of dos and don'ts based not on Scripture but on tradition or personal preference—then they judge themselves and others on their performance. In a nutshell, it's "checklist Christianity."

B. How does it appear? Legalism slips unnoticed into the church like a deadly enemy cloaked in pious, religious garb. When it does, the Bridegroom's party grows suddenly silent... the wine turns quickly back to water... and joy in the Christian life soon loses its festive flavor. Legalists prey on churches and Christians—especially on young, biblically naive believers. Paul describes legalists in Galatians 2:4 as "false brethren who had sneaked in to spy out our liberty which we have in Christ Jesus, in order to bring us into bondage."

C. Why is it wrong? First and foremost, legalism is unbiblical. Grace and freedom are the hallmarks of the Christian life

(John 8:32, Rom. 8:1–2, 1 Cor. 8), not law and bondage (Gal. 2). Second, it promotes the flesh, which cannot please God (Rom. 8:8). Third, it is based on pride, a prime example of which is the parable of the Pharisee and the tax gatherer.

> And He also told this parable to certain ones who trusted in themselves that they were righteous, and viewed others with contempt: "Two men went up into the temple to pray, one a Pharisee, and the other a tax-gatherer. The Pharisee stood and was praying thus to himself, 'God, I thank Thee that I am not like other people: swindlers, unjust, adulterers, or even like this tax-gatherer. I fast twice a week; I pay tithes of all that I get.' But the tax-gatherer, standing some distance away, was even unwilling to lift up his eyes to heaven, but was beating his breast, saying, 'God, be merciful to me, the sinner!' I tell you, this man went down to his house justified rather than the other; for he who humbles himself shall be exalted." (Luke 18:9–14)

Like an ornate Corinthian column in the temple where the Pharisee prayed, a proud, erect "I" is the pillar that supports legalism.

A Balanced Perspective

Law and grace are opposite living standards. But this does not mean that there was no grace for those who lived under the Law . . . nor that there are no laws for us, who live under grace (see Exod. 20:5–6; Ps. 51:1; Rom. 8:2; Gal. 6:2; James 1:25, 2:8).

Grace never promotes a do-as-you-please philosophy or a loose life of selfishness, sinfulness, and licentiousness. Romans 6:12–18 confirms this fact. The major differences, however, between living under the Law and living under grace lie with the recipients of the commands and their motivation to obey.

The Israelites received the Mosaic Law and its more than six hundred commands. They were motivated to obey by *fear* and empowered only by the *flesh*. Today, believers in Jesus Christ receive grace. Although the New Testament also contains hundreds of commands, we are motivated by *love* and empowered by the *Holy Spirit*.

What motivates your obedience to Christ—law and fear, or the grace and love now offered us?

D. When did it start? Legalism is an ancient art, begun by the Pharisees and implemented by subsequent generations of apprentices who have been narrow, rigid, and often intolerably religious. Legalists have refused to accept the doctrine of sheer grace. Instead, they have sought to supplement grace with the mingled alloy of their own works. To this day, pockets of legalism thrive in every corner of the country and in almost every church.

II. Legalism: Let's Examine It

The pivotal issue on which the controversy in John 5 turns is the question of observing the Sabbath. Before we get into that passage, let's do a little spadework to uncover the Sabbath's biblical and traditional roots.

A. Background information. Three pieces of history shed considerable light on the Sabbath and what it means.

1. **Origin of the Sabbath.** At the end of Genesis 1, we read that God completed His work of creation in six days. In 2:2, Moses states: "And by the seventh day God completed His work which He had done; and He rested...." Essentially, *sabbath* means rest, translated from the Hebrew term *shabath.*

2. **Law of the Sabbath.** In Exodus 20, the Law God gave to Moses required observance of the Sabbath, and He based His injunction on the pattern of the creation.

   "Remember the sabbath day, to keep it holy. Six days you shall labor and do all your work, but the seventh day is a sabbath of the Lord your God; in it you shall not do any work, you or your son or your daughter, your male or your female servant or your cattle or your sojourner who stays with you. For in six days the Lord made the heavens and the earth, the sea and all that is in them, and rested on the seventh day; therefore the Lord blessed the sabbath day and made it holy." (vv. 8–11)

3. **Tradition of the Sabbath.** Slipping in between the Old and New Testaments, the Pharisees amplified the Sabbath law by adding thirty-nine categories of unpermitted work, along with a number of tedious restrictions. These became part of the traditional teachings of the rabbis, who then enforced them among the people. Yet these requirements stretched considerably beyond God's original intent. For example, notice how obsessive the restrictions had become in just this one regulation.

If a man removed his finger-nails by means of his nails or his teeth, and so, too, if [he pulled out] the hair of his head, or his moustache or his beard; and so, too, if a woman dressed her hair or painted her eyelids or reddened [her face]—such a one [Rabbi] Eliezer declares liable [to a Sin-offering]. (Shab. 10:6)[1]

So much for men biting their nails or women fixing their hair on the way to the synagogue!

B. Biblical exposition: healing the sick. Now that we understand the Pharisees' legalistic view of the Sabbath, let's turn to a story in John 5 that shows how they valued their traditional principles more than people.

1. **The need** (vv. 1–5). The opening scene is squalid; the stench, repulsive; the circumstances, depressing.

> After these things there was a feast of the Jews, and Jesus went up to Jerusalem. Now there is in Jerusalem by the sheep gate a pool, which is called in Hebrew Bethesda, having five porticoes. In these lay a multitude of those who were sick, blind, lame, and withered, [waiting for the moving of the waters; for an angel of the Lord went down at certain seasons into the pool, and stirred up the water; whoever then first, after the stirring up of the water, stepped in was made well from whatever disease with which he was afflicted.] And a certain man was there, who had been thirty-eight years in his sickness.

For thirty-eight years, this pathetic, bruised reed of a man has lain here in the poverty, the repulsion, and the despair. Yet within him flickers a dimly burning wick of hope.

2. **The miracle** (vv. 6–9a). It was just such "bruised reeds" and "dimly burning wicks" that Jesus the servant came to help and to heal (see Isa. 42:1–3). With the tender compassion of a child choosing the runt of the litter, Jesus gives special attention to this withered man.

> When Jesus saw him lying there, and knew that he had already been a long time in that condition, He said to him, "Do you wish to get well?" The sick man answered Him, "Sir, I have no man to put me into the pool when the water is stirred up, but while I am coming, another steps down before me." Jesus said to him, "Arise, take up

1. *The Mishnah,* trans. Herbert Danby (Oxford, England: Oxford University Press, 1933), p. 110.

71

your pallet, and walk." And immediately the man became well, and took up his pallet and began to walk.

Walking Away from Bethesda

Just as distance was no barrier to healing the royal official's son, so time was no obstacle for Jesus to overcome in healing the lame man. Thirty-eight years of misery, shame, embarrassment, and despair . . . in a split second, that was all history.

No matter how miserable your life has been—no matter how lame your spiritual life or how long you've been limping—Jesus can change it. The real question is: Do you wish to get well?

It's easy to become accustomed to life around the pool of misery. The peer group there certainly won't criticize you. People will make space for your pallet and then leave you to yourself—or even commiserate with you.

But maybe, after years of inner poverty, you're looking for a change, longing to be restored to everything God created you to be. If so, Jesus is the ticket out of that slum. If you *really* want to get well, He'll give you the grace and strength to take up your pallet and walk.

---

3. **The confrontation** (vv. 9b–17). Notice how quickly this sunny moment of joy is muted by the gray shadows of legalism.

> Now it was the Sabbath on that day. Therefore the Jews were saying to him who was cured, "It is the Sabbath, and it is not permissible for you to carry your pallet." (vv. 9b–10)

Undoubtedly, the witnesses around the pool are bustling with excitement. But the miracle leaves the legalists bristling with anger. When they should have been on their knees in praise, the only thing these Pharisees can do is pull out their principle-book and quote condemnation, chapter and verse. And in the midst of their straining the gnat from their list of pure regulations, Jesus slips through the sieve.

> But [the man] answered them, "He who made me well was the one who said to me, 'Take up your pallet and walk.'" They asked him, "Who is the man who said to you, 'Take up your pallet, and walk'?" But he who was healed did not know

who it was; for Jesus had slipped away while there was a crowd in that place. Afterward Jesus found him in the temple, and said to him, "Behold, you have become well; do not sin anymore, so that nothing worse may befall you." The man went away, and told the Jews that it was Jesus who had made him well. And for this reason the Jews were persecuting Jesus, because He was doing these things on the Sabbath. But He answered them, "My Father is working until now, and I Myself am working." (vv. 11–17)

4. **The reaction** (v. 18). When the Jews hear of Jesus' escape and His testimony to the healed man, they are livid.

For this cause therefore the Jews were seeking all the more to kill Him, because He not only was breaking the Sabbath, but also was calling God His own Father, making Himself equal with God. (v. 18)

Essentially, the indictments of the legalists were twofold: one, Jesus broke the Sabbath (vv. 16, 18); two, Jesus claimed equality with God by claiming Him as His Father (vv. 17–18). Ironically, the Pharisees were the guilty ones: they judged Jesus, refused to rejoice or give praise at the healing, and even went so far as to plot Christ's assassination.

III. Legalism: Let's Avoid It

We must keep legalism from gaining a foothold in our lives and churches. To oppose legalism, *truth* must emerge. Paul confronted legalism, refusing to look the other way (see Gal. 2:14, 4:16). To combat legalism, *conviction* must be employed. This may even mean taking a stand with a good friend or a spiritual leader, as Paul did with Peter when that church rock began to crumble under legalism's heavy weight (see Gal. 2:11–14). To overcome legalism, *grace* must be embraced. Works and our obsequious duty to them will never be abandoned until we reach out for God's grace—and as we do, the shackles of legalism will fall from our wrists and ankles. Then and only then will we be truly free.

"For through the Law I died to the Law, that I might live to God. I have been crucified with Christ; and it is no longer I who live, but Christ lives in me; and the life which I now live in the flesh I live by faith in the Son of God, who loved me, and delivered Himself up for me." (Gal. 2:19–20)

🌳 *Living Insights*

Legalism is destructive—it denies the grace of God, exalts self, and promotes pride. Let's continue our study of legalism by looking at Paul's epistle to the Galatians.

- Read through Galatians' six chapters. In the following space, record statements you find concerning legalism, mixing law and grace, or adding works to faith. You'll find a bundle of them in this small but potent epistle.

Galatians: An Exposé of Legalism

Reference: _____

Significant statement: _____

_____

Reference: _____

Significant statement: _____

_____

Reference: _____

Significant statement: _____

_____

Reference: _____

Significant statement: _____

_____

Reference: _____

Significant statement: _____

_____

Reference: _____

Significant statement: _____

_____

🌳 Living Insights

Not only does Galatians give us statements of truth concerning the issue of legalism, it also gives us practical ways to combat this dangerous attitude. Let's use this time to discover these strategies.

- Reread the letter to the Galatians, paying particular attention to how to fight legalism. Paul offers many suggestions. Note your findings in the space provided.

Galatians: How to Fight Legalism

Reference: _____

Strategy: _____

_____

Reference: _____

Strategy: _____

_____

Reference: _____

Strategy: _____

_____

Reference: _____

Strategy: _____

_____

Reference: _____

Strategy: _____

_____

Reference: _____

Strategy: _____

_____

The Claims of the Christ
John 5:17–30

In the early 1950s, Boris Nicholayevich Kornfeld, a Jewish medical doctor, was sentenced to a Russian concentration camp, ostensibly for some minor political crime. Because of his training, Kornfeld became a prison surgeon, operating on both fellow prisoners and hated guards in poorly lit, unsanitary conditions. Stripped of his possessions and dignity, as well as his faith in the political system, Kornfeld was led to Jesus by a kind, educated inmate. For the first time, he saw that salvation was not through communism but through Christ.

In that dank, catacomb existence, the seed of faith planted by that one prisoner began to germinate and spread its roots deep into Kornfeld's soul. The doctor could no longer ignore the corruption that filled the prison—the suffering, violence, thefts, and lies. For him, faith was not a wall plaque or bumper sticker; it was a life-changing commitment to the Savior who came to alleviate suffering and rectify injustice. Because he no longer cooperated with their dishonest schemes, Kornfeld increasingly angered those in charge.

It came to a head the day he turned in an orderly caught stealing bread from patients dying of malnutrition. His superiors smiled secretly, for they knew that anyone who dared snitch on another inmate would not live long.

At the same time, Kornfeld was assigned a new patient—a young man with a melon-shaped head, empty eyes, and a childlike expression. As Kornfeld cared for this desperately ill patient, he talked about his new freedom in Christ. Although the man drifted in and out of consciousness, the doctor's zeal caught his attention. The patient knew he was hearing about an incredible transformation, and he hung onto the doctor's every word until, at last, he fell asleep.

The next morning the patient was wakened by the sound of running feet and loud noises. In hushed whispers, another patient told him that someone had crept up on the sleeping doctor and crushed his head with a mallet. The "stoolie" had been silenced.

But Kornfeld's testimony lived on. And it forever changed the life of that one young man with the melon-shaped head and the empty eyes. He survived his illness and the concentration camp and lived to tell the world what he had learned there.

The patient? Alexander Solzhenitsyn.[1]

---

1. Story retold from the account in Chuck Colson's *Loving God* (Grand Rapids, Mich.: Zondervan Publishing House, 1983), pp. 27–34.

Kornfeld and Solzhenitsyn learned a lesson we can apply today—the claims of Christ were never meant to merely adorn our coat lapels or emblazon our car bumpers. They were meant to make changes in our lives and in the lives of those around us—changes as radical as the claims themselves, which we will examine in our study of John 5.

I. Background
Preceding Christ's remarkable claims was the miraculous healing of a man who had been sick for thirty-eight years (John 5:1–9a). But the Jews' reactions scandalized this merciful act because it took place on the Sabbath (vv. 9b–17). In His response, Jesus claims equality with the Father and incurs a whirlwind of religious wrath.

II. Discourse
In the calm eye of this gathering storm of criticism and treachery, Jesus begins a discourse that is life-changing in its implications.

A. General answer (vv. 17–18). Replying to the Pharisees' accusations, Jesus makes some amazing claims, the first of which is general in nature.

> "My Father is working until now, and I Myself am working." (v. 17)

As the following verse reveals, this claim sets in motion a backlash of resistance.

> For this cause therefore the Jews were seeking all the more to kill Him, because He not only was breaking the Sabbath, but also was calling God His own Father, making Himself equal with God. (v. 18)

B. Specific claims (vv. 19–30). Moving from the general to the specific, Jesus' claims become not only more profound but more pointed as well.

> 1. **"I am equal with God"** (vv. 19–20). Throughout the passage, Jesus never refers to God generically as *our* Father. It is always *My* Father or *the* Father (see vv. 17, 19). In doing so, He claims a unique relationship with God. The Jews recognize the implications of the claim: that in "calling God His own Father," Jesus is "making Himself equal with God" (v. 18b). And Jesus claims not only an equal relationship with God but also equality in the work they share.

> "Truly, truly, I say to you, the Son can do nothing of Himself, unless it is something He sees the Father doing; for whatever the Father does, these things the Son also does in like manner. For the Father loves the Son, and shows Him all things that He Himself is doing; and greater works than these will He show Him, that you may marvel." (vv. 19–20)

Like a shadow, which is neither identical to nor independent of the substance from which it is cast, so the Son and the Father are distinct from, yet dependent upon, each other.
2. **"I am the giver of life"** (vv. 21, 26). An example of the "greater works" in verse 20 is given in verses 21 and 26.

> "For just as the Father raises the dead and gives them life, even so the Son also gives life to whom He wishes.... For just as the Father has life in Himself, even so He gave to the Son also to have life in Himself."

To assert His equality, Jesus claims to have the same power the Father does over the dead. This statement comes from the germinal seed of truth buried in John's prologue, stating that "in Him was life" (1:4). It finds its fruition in the raising of Lazarus in chapter 11. While many may claim the power to heal, no one but Christ claims the ability to raise the dead.

The Gift of Life

Man can give medicine when sickness comes,
    food when hunger comes,
    help when weakness comes,
    love when loneliness comes.
But when death comes, man can give
    only sympathy,
    only compassion,
Never the gift of life.
    Only God can do that.

---

3. **"I am the final judge"** (vv. 22–23). Delivering perhaps His most striking claim thus far, Jesus curls their toes with this one.

> "For not even the Father judges anyone, but He has given all judgment to the Son." (v. 22)

Most people mistakenly believe that God the Father is the final judge of mankind. But this verse, along with many others in the New Testament, indicates that Jesus will be the judge (see Acts 10:42, 2 Cor. 5:10, 2 Tim. 4:1). And just as a judge is esteemed as Your Honor, and all participants rise when he enters the courtroom, so it is only fitting that the highest judge, enthroned at the right hand of God the Father, should receive such honor from His creatures.

4. **"I determine man's destiny"** (v. 24). Not only does Jesus claim to be the judge, He claims to be the ticket out of the courtroom for any who stand guilty.

> "Truly, truly, I say to you, he who hears My word, and believes Him who sent Me, has eternal life, and does not come into judgment, but has passed out of death into life."

The words "truly, truly" ring out like a town crier's "hear ye, hear ye," drawing attention to this important message. It is important because it carries good news: eternal life without the threat of judgment. But first, two things are required of man: a hearing ear and a believing heart. Anyone who accepts this gift by faith buries forever the fear of eternal separation from God (Rom. 8:1, 38–39).

5. **"I will raise the dead"** (vv. 25–29). In another dramatic "hear ye, hear ye" announcement, Jesus gives us some of the Bible's clearest information regarding resurrection.

> "Truly, truly, I say to you, an hour is coming and now is, when the dead shall hear the voice of the Son of God; and those who hear shall live. For just as the Father has life in Himself, even so He gave to the Son also to have life in Himself; and He gave Him authority to execute judgment, because He is the Son of Man. Do not marvel at this; for an hour is coming, in which all who are in the tombs shall hear His voice, and shall come

forth; those who did the good deeds to a resurrection of life, those who committed the evil deeds to a resurrection of judgment."

Three crystal-clear facts surface regarding the final judgment: (1) there will definitely be life after death; (2) every person will be affected by it; and (3) mankind will fall into two, and only two, categories. Though these facts shine through, some have found verse 29 a little confusing. Taken by itself, it seems to indicate that eternal destiny is based on our deeds—good or evil—rather than on belief or unbelief. But as we study John's writings, it's clear that he saw "doing good" as a natural outgrowth of the saving gospel's seed planted in the heart of the believer at the time of the new birth.

Beloved, do not imitate what is evil, but what is good. The one who does good is of God; the one who does evil has not seen God. (3 John 11)

From the viewpoint of the gospel writers, the "good" life emerges through a relationship with Christ, and the "evil" life encroaches through separation from Him (compare Matt. 25:31–46).

6. **"I am always doing the will of God"** (v. 30). As a shadow does not move on its own initiative, so Jesus moves only in cadence with the Father's footsteps.

"I can do nothing on My own initiative. As I hear, I judge; and My judgment is just, because I do not seek My own will, but the will of Him who sent Me."

This verse finds an echo in chapter 8.

Jesus therefore said, "When you lift up the Son of Man, then you will know that I am He, and I do nothing on My own initiative, but I speak these things as the Father taught Me. And He who sent Me is with Me; He has not left Me alone, for I always do the things that are pleasing to Him." (vv. 28–29)

Taking to Heart the Claims of Christ

The claims of Christ are so radical that they cry out for an equally radical commitment to Him.

The nameless prisoner who shared the claims of Christ with Dr. Boris Kornfeld made such a commitment.

For Kornfeld, too, the revolutionary claims of Christ,

80

which stood in sharp relief against the moral bankruptcy of communism, elicited such a commitment.

And in the frightened young Solzhenitsyn, whose life teetered between heaven and hell in a prison hospital ward, there developed such a commitment.

How about you? Have Christ's radical claims made any radical changes in your life?

Living Insights

Study One

During Christ's earthly life, no one could mistake His claims as Lord. That is an important fact to consider when drawing a conclusion as to who Jesus really is. The fifth chapter of John's Gospel strongly addresses the issue of Christ's deity. Let's examine it further.

• Earlier in this study guide we used paraphrasing to make the text come alive. Let's use that method again with John 5:17–30. Remember, the advantage of paraphrasing is capturing the feelings of the characters and the meanings of their words. Try to catch the impact of Christ's claims to deity.

John 5:17–30 . . . A Paraphrase

_____

_____

_____

_____

_____

_____

_____

_____

_____

_____

_____

_____

Continued on next page

81

_____

_____

_____

_____

_____

_____

_____

_____

_____

_____

_____

Living Insights

Study Two ▬▬▬▬▬▬▬▬▬▬▬▬▬▬▬▬▬▬▬▬▬▬▬▬

Have you paused in the busyness of your schedule to give thanks to God for His marvelous work in your life? We cannot interact with the claims of Christ's deity without being humbled by the fact that the great, almighty God is present within all believers. We have so much for which to be grateful.

- Thank the Lord for all His blessings. He's done a lot for you, hasn't He? Acknowledge His lordship in your life, and be specific about what that really means. Make this prayer time a time of appreciation, not a time of request. Don't ask God for anything; just thank Him for what you have already received.

Witnesses for the Defense

John 5:31–47

Mark Lane was an attorney who defended a dead man—and got results.

His client? Lee Harvey Oswald, accused assassin of President John F. Kennedy. But before Lane could even begin preparing his defense, Oswald, too, was shot and killed. Another attorney might have closed the case, but not Mark Lane. In fact, he worked harder than ever to prove that his deceased client had not acted alone in the presidential assassination plot.

Lane documented his findings in the best-selling book *Rush to Judgment.* The facts, interviews, and pictures he gathered cast a convincing shadow of doubt over the single-assassin theory. So influential was the book that public opinion shifted, causing 69 percent of the people polled to disagree with the accepted view that a lone assassin was responsible for the president's death.

Why was the single-assassin theory questioned? How was the public swayed? Through the use of key witnesses.

In a similar manner, Jesus marshaled key witnesses to His defense when the Pharisees accused Him of being a Sabbath breaker and a blasphemer.

I. Bearing Witness: The Law

The fifth chapter of John's Gospel provides us with a drama in three vignettes. First, a *miracle,* where a man paralyzed for thirty-eight years is instantly healed. Second, a *series of claims,* where Jesus Christ testifies that He is the Son of God. Third, a *defense,* where five witnesses are introduced to verify His claims. To begin His defense, Jesus makes a startling statement.

> "If I alone bear witness of Myself, My testimony is not true." (v. 31)

A. Meaning of the statement. Jesus does not mean that His claims are false, only that His testimony alone would not be valid in a court of law. According to rabbinic sayings and Jewish procedure, "none may be believed when he testifies of himself."[1]

B. Reason for the statement. According to Jewish law, even a single witness was insufficient to determine the truth of a matter.

> "A single witness shall not rise up against a man on account of any iniquity or any sin which he has committed; on the evidence of two or three witnesses a matter shall be confirmed." (Deut. 19:15)

---

1. Leon Morris, *The Gospel According to John* (Grand Rapids, Mich.: William B. Eerdmans Publishing Co., 1971), p. 324, fn. 91.

II. Hearing the Witnesses: Their Testimonies

In John 5:32–47, the Lord appeals to five witnesses in His defense. Imagine yourself as a juror and Jesus on trial as the defendant. The first witness is called.

A. Witness number one: God the Father.

> "There is another who bears witness of Me, and I know that the testimony which He bears of Me is true." (v. 32)

Two grammatical points in the original Greek add color to this verse. To begin with, notice how Jesus introduces the Father: "There is another." The word *another* in the Greek means "another of the same kind."[2] It is a subtle reference to deity (compare 14:16, where He uses the same word to describe the Holy Spirit). The second point is that the Greek construction for the verb "bears witness" indicates continual action. The Father continually testifies to the claims of Christ. At Jesus' birth, the Father announced the arrival with prophets, angels, and a miraculous star. At Jesus' baptism, the Father testified: "This is My beloved Son, in whom I am well-pleased" (Matt. 3:17b). And, later in Jesus' life, the Father reaffirms His own testimony—at the Transfiguration (17:5), the Crucifixion (27:51–54), the Resurrection (28:1–7), and the Ascension (Acts 1:9–11). In a searing rebuke, Jesus underscores this testimony to His accusers.

> "And the Father who sent Me, He has borne witness of Me. You have neither heard His voice at any time, nor seen His form. And you do not have His word abiding in you, for you do not believe Him whom He sent." (John 5:37–38)

B. Witness number two: John the forerunner.
Jesus next calls John the Baptist to the witness stand.

> "You have sent to John, and he has borne witness to the truth. But the witness which I receive is not from man, but I say these things that you may be saved. He was the lamp that was burning and was shining and you were willing to rejoice for a while in his light." (vv. 33–35)

True to form, John the Baptist's testimony is clear and simple. The next day he saw Jesus coming to him, and said, "Behold, the Lamb of God who takes away the sin of the world! This is He on behalf of whom I said, 'After me comes a Man who has a higher rank than I, for He existed before me.' And I did not recognize Him,

---

2. The Greek word is *allos.* Its near cousin is the word *heteros,* meaning "another of a different kind."

but in order that He might be manifested to Israel, I came baptizing in water." And John bore witness saying, "I have beheld the Spirit descending as a dove out of heaven, and He remained upon Him. And I did not recognize Him, but He who sent me to baptize in water said to me, 'He upon whom you see the Spirit descending and remaining upon Him, this is the one who baptizes in the Holy Spirit.' And I have seen, and have borne witness that this is the Son of God." (1:29–34)

Like moths flitting near a candle, these Jews had swarmed around John—that is, until they got too close to the flame. Then, one by one, they took flight. The light, they liked. It was the heat that drove them away.

C. Witness number three: Jesus' own works. The defense now moves from verbal to visual evidence. Verse 36 of chapter 5 presents Exhibit A.

"But the witness which I have is greater than that of John; for the works which the Father has given Me to accomplish, the very works that I do, bear witness of Me, that the Father has sent Me."

John's Gospel provides irrefutable evidence for Christ's divinity. He has already turned water into the finest of aged wines, healed a government official's son long-distance, and restored a paralytic. In the pages that follow, He will miraculously feed five thousand, walk on water, heal a blind man, and raise Lazarus from the dead. Jesus' works speak for themselves, yet the defense doesn't rest. Instead, Jesus calls forth another witness.

D. Witness number four: the Scriptures.

"You search the Scriptures, because you think that in them you have eternal life; and it is these that bear witness of Me; and you are unwilling to come to Me, that you may have life. I do not receive glory from men; but I know you, that you do not have the love of God in yourselves. I have come in My Father's name, and you do not receive Me; if another shall come in his own name, you will receive him. How can you believe, when you receive glory from one another, and you do not seek the glory that is from the one and only God?" (vv. 39–44)

These rigid literalists couldn't see the Messiah because God's Word was not truly abiding in them and God's Son was not the object of their faith. The Old Testament Scriptures megaphoned news of the coming Messiah (see Luke 24:27, 44; Acts 8:30–35). But these Jews turned a deaf ear (Luke 13:34).[3]

Some Personal Application

It's easy to skate on the cold, impersonal outer surfaces of life—to get caught up in the technical, the peripheral, the superficial.

For a lawyer trafficking in the legal maze, it's easy to become enamored with the intricacies of the law and yet never develop a heart for justice.

For a doctor, it's easy to become swept up in the swirl of state-of-the-art medicine and never develop a heart of compassion.

For the professional minister or the serious student of the Scriptures, it's easy to become enraptured with exegesis instead of Jesus, carrying on a love affair with the printed page rather than with the person of Christ.

The Bible was given not simply as a legal document or a self-help book but as a love letter. And if that letter doesn't draw us irresistibly toward Christ, then it's possible that we, like those prosecutorial Jews, do not have His Word abiding in us.

E. Witness number five: Moses. Jesus now turns the courtroom tables and points an indicting finger at His litigious accusers.

> "Do not think that I will accuse you before the Father; the one who accuses you is Moses, in whom you have set your hope. For if you believed Moses, you would believe Me; for he wrote of Me. But if you do not believe his writings, how will you believe My words?"
> (John 5:45–47)

As His trump card, Jesus pulls an ace out of the deck of Jewish heroes: Moses. Why Moses? Because, like Abraham, Isaac, and Joseph, Moses was one of the founding fathers of Judaism. He

---

3. "After the destruction of the temple of Solomon in 586 B.C., the Jewish scholars of the Exile substituted the study of the Law for the observance of the temple ritual and sacrifices. They pored over the OT, endeavoring to extract the fullest possible meaning from its words, because they believed that the very study itself would bring them life. By so doing they missed the chief subject of the OT revelation. Jesus claimed the Law, the Prophets, and the Psalms (Writings) as witnesses to his person and claims (Luke 24:44). He rebuked his hearers for their inconsistency in studying the Scriptures so diligently while rejecting his claims, which were founded on those same Scriptures." Merrill C. Tenney, "The Gospel of John," *The Expositor's Bible Commentary*, vol. 9 (Grand Rapids, Mich.: The Zondervan Corp., 1981), p. 68.

spearheaded the Exodus, gave them the Law, and was looked up to with reverence. But when did Moses ever write of Christ? Turn back to the prophetic pages of Deuteronomy 18.

> "The Lord your God will raise up for you a prophet like me from among you, from your countrymen, you shall listen to him. . . . 'And it shall come about that whoever will not listen to My words which he shall speak in My name, I Myself will require it of him.' "
> (vv. 15, 19)

But how can we be sure Jesus was "the prophet" referred to by Moses? Read Peter's words in Acts 3. Notice that he quotes the passage from Deuteronomy.

> "But the things which God announced beforehand by the mouth of all the prophets, that His Christ should suffer, He has thus fulfilled. Repent therefore and return, that your sins may be wiped away, in order that times of refreshing may come from the presence of the Lord; and that He may send Jesus, the Christ appointed for you, whom heaven must receive until the period of restoration of all things about which God spoke by the mouth of His holy prophets from ancient time. Moses said, 'The Lord God shall raise up for you a prophet like me from your brethren; to Him you shall give heed in everything He says to you. And it shall be that every soul that does not heed that prophet shall be utterly destroyed from among the people.' " (vv. 18–23)

III. The Verdict: A Serious Choice

The witnesses have been carefully chosen. Each has taken the stand. The evidence has been judiciously presented. The defense rests. As a member of the jury, you must deliberate. You must weigh the evidence. It's a sobering decision, for the verdict you reach about Christ is a serious one. It is, quite literally, a matter of life or death— *your* life or *your* death.

Continued on next page

Living Insights

When we conclude a study like this, perhaps the most important thing we can do is take some time to review what we have learned through the last twelve lessons.

- Listed below are the titles of the twelve lessons we have studied. Go back through your study guide, notes, and Bible to find the most important *truth* you discovered in each lesson.

Exalting Christ . . . The Son of God

"That You May Believe"_____

_____

_____

Prelude to Deity _____

_____

_____

A Man Sent from God _____

_____

_____

Five Who Followed in Faith _____

_____

_____

Wine . . . Coins . . . and Signs_____

_____

_____

Brainstorming the New Birth _____

_____

_____

The Preacher Who Lost His Congregation _____

_____

_____

Water for a Thirsty Woman _____

_____

_____

Healing at a Distance _____

_____

_____

An Exposé of Legalism _____

_____

_____

The Claims of the Christ _____

_____

_____

Witnesses for the Defense _____

_____

_____

 *Living Insights*

Study Two ━━━━━━━━━━━━━━━━━━━━━━━━━━━━━━━━━━━━━

Let's continue our review of the first five chapters of John's Gospel. This time, we'll direct our attention to the applications we made during our time together.

- Page back through your notes and look for the most significant *applications* you made from each of the lessons. Record your answers in the space provided.

Exalting Christ . . . The Son of God

"That You May Believe" _____

_____

_____

Continued on next page

Prelude to Deity _____

_____

_____

A Man Sent from God _____

_____

_____

Five Who Followed in Faith _____

_____

_____

Wine . . . Coins . . . and Signs_____

_____

_____

Brainstorming the New Birth _____

_____

_____

The Preacher Who Lost His Congregation _____

_____

_____

Water for a Thirsty Woman _____

_____

_____

Healing at a Distance _____

_____

_____

An Exposé of Legalism _____

_____

_____

The Claims of the Christ _____

_____

_____

Witnesses for the Defense _____

_____

_____

Books for Probing Further

"In the beginning was the Word, and the Word was with God, and the Word was God.... And the Word became flesh, and dwelt among us, and we beheld His glory, glory as of the only begotten from the Father, full of grace and truth" (John 1:1, 14).

Deity was never so awesome
As when it nursed from a young maiden's breast.
No pomp. No pageantry.
No flash. No fanfare.
God slipped unpretentiously into the warm lake of humanity,
With barely a ripple of notice.
In His wake
A quiet greatness
Moved in concentric circles,
Touching everyone He met:
    a fisherman, weathered and worn;
    a woman, Samaritan and shameful;
    a man, thirty-eight years lame.
A rolled-up pallet,
An empty waterpot,
Nets hung out to dry,
Forever left behind
    for Him,
        who was full of grace and truth;
    for Him,
        whose brimming glory
        spilled into their empty lives.
Where there was meaningless labor,
    He gave mission.
Where there was thirst for forgiveness,
    He gave living water.
Where there was hurt,
    He gave healing.
Deity was never so winsome
As when the Light of the World
    touched these dimly burning wicks,
    and gave them a reason to shine.

—Ken Gire

We hope these first studies in John have helped *your* light shine a little brighter and a little warmer for Christ and that His winsome ways will fan the flame of your spiritual passion. To further feed that fire, we recommend the following books.

I. Commentaries

Morris, Leon. *Commentary on the Gospel of John.* Grand Rapids, Mich.: William B. Eerdmans Publishing Co., 1971. Probably the best commentary on John available, this comprehensive study serves the interests of student and scholar alike. Its exposition is highly readable and well researched, while the more technical points are relegated to footnotes.

————. *The Word Made Flesh: John 1–5,* volume 1 of *Reflections on the Gospel of John.* Grand Rapids, Mich.: Baker Book House, 1986. Writing with a light touch but with the weight of scholarship, the author expounds the text of John's Gospel in a most arresting way, weaving together theology, history, exegesis, illustration, and application. A layman's commentary that can be read like a book.

Pink, Arthur. *Exposition of the Gospel of John.* Grand Rapids, Mich.: Zondervan Publishing House, 1945. Although somewhat allegorical in its interpretations, this commentary is the fruit of years of meditation by the author and serves as a good, nontechnical companion to Morris's commentaries.

II. Apologetic Studies

Little, Paul. *Know What You Believe.* Wheaton, Ill.: Victor Books, 1987. This best-selling classic presents a practical discussion of the fundamentals of the faith, explaining what the Bible teaches about God, Jesus, Christ's death and resurrection, the Holy Spirit, God's Word, and other critical topics.

————. *Know Why You Believe.* Wheaton, Ill.: Victor Books, 1987. Affirming the reasonableness of the Christian faith is the purpose of this book. As a valuable resource, it will help you gain confidence in sharing your faith with others.

III. General Interest

Bruce, A. B. *The Training of the Twelve.* Grand Rapids, Mich.: Kregel Publications, 1971. A study of the disciples, their personalities, their development, and the teachings they received from Jesus, based on the Gospel records. The late Bible teacher W. H. Griffith Thomas called this work one of the great classics of the nineteenth century.

Hodges, Zane C. *The Hungry Inherit.* Chicago, Ill.: Moody Press, 1973. A creative exposition of John 4 and the woman at the well, this excellent book will expand your understanding of many New Testament principles and the meaning of salvation, discipleship, and rewards.

Insight for Living
Cassette Tapes
EXALTING CHRIST ... THE SON OF GOD
A STUDY OF JOHN 1–5

Here are twelve cassette messages that present the facts regarding Christ's deity. In simple, easy-to-understand terms, each message reveals convincing proof from the biblical text that Jesus of Nazareth was, in fact, undiminished deity in human flesh.

			U.S.	Canadian
ECS	CS	Cassette series—includes album cover	$34.50	$43.75
		Individual cassettes—include messages		
		A and B	5.00	6.35

These prices are effective as of September 1987 and are subject to change without notice.

ECS   1-A: *"That You May Believe"*
        Survey of John
      B: *Prelude to Deity*
        John 1:1–18

ECS   2-A: *A Man Sent from God*
        John 1:6–8, 15, 19–34
      B: *Five Who Followed in Faith*
        John 1:35–51

ECS   3-A: *Wine . . . Coins . . . and Signs*
        John 2
      B: *Brainstorming the New Birth*
        John 3:1–21

ECS   4-A: *The Preacher Who Lost His Congregation*
        John 3:22–36
      B: *Water for a Thirsty Woman*
        John 4:1–42

ECS   5-A: *Healing at a Distance*
        John 4:46–54
      B: *An Exposé of Legalism*
        John 5:1–18

ECS   6-A: *The Claims of the Christ*
        John 5:17–30
      B: *Witnesses for the Defense*
        John 5:31–47

Ordering Information

U.S. ordering information: You are welcome to use our toll-free number (for Visa and MasterCard orders only) between the hours of 8:30 A.M. and 4:00 P.M., Pacific time, Monday through Friday. The number is **(800) 772-8888.** This number may be used anywhere in the United States except California, Hawaii, and Alaska. Orders from these areas are handled through our Sales Department at **(714) 870-9161.** We are unable to accept collect calls.

Your order will be processed promptly. We ask that you allow four to six weeks for delivery by fourth-class mail. If you wish your order to be shipped first-class, please add 10 percent of the total order cost (not including California sales tax) for shipping and handling.

Canadian ordering information: Your order will be processed promptly. We ask that you allow approximately four weeks for delivery. All orders will be shipped from our Canadian office. For our listeners in British Columbia, a 6 percent sales tax must be added to the total of all tape orders (not including postage). For further information, please contact our office at **(604) 272-5811.**

Payment options: We accept personal checks, money orders, Visa, and MasterCard in payment for materials ordered. Unfortunately, we are unable to offer invoicing or COD orders. If the amount of your check or money order is less than the amount of your purchase, your check will be returned so that you may place your order again with the correct amount. All orders must be paid in full before shipment can be made.

Returned checks: There is a $10 charge for any returned check (regardless of the amount of your order) to cover processing and invoicing.

Guarantee: Our tapes are guaranteed for ninety days against faulty performance or breakage due to a defect in the tape. For best results, please be sure your tape recorder is in good operating condition and is cleaned regularly.

Mail your order to one of the following addresses:

Insight for Living
Sales Department
Post Office Box 4444
Fullerton, CA 92634

Insight for Living Ministries
Post Office Box 2510
Vancouver, BC
Canada V6B 3W7

Quantity discounts and gift certificates are available upon request.

Overseas Ordering Information

If you do not live in the United States or Canada, please note the following information. This will ensure efficient processing of your request.

Estimated time of delivery: We ask that you allow approximately twelve to sixteen weeks for delivery by surface mail. If you would like your order sent airmail, the length of delivery may be reduced. All orders will be shipped from our office in Fullerton, California.

Payment options: Due to fluctuating currency rates, we can accept only personal checks made payable in U.S. funds, international money orders, Visa, and MasterCard in payment for materials ordered. If the amount of your check or money order is less than the amount of your purchase, your check will be returned so that you may place your order again with the correct amount. All orders must be paid in full before shipment can be made.

Returned checks: There is a $10 charge for any returned check (regardless of the amount of your order) to cover processing and invoicing.

Postage and handling: Please add to the amount of purchase the postage cost for the service you desire. All orders must include postage based on the chart below.

Purchase Amount		Surface Postage	Airmail Postage
From	To	Percentage of Order	Percentage of Order
$ .01	$15.00	40%	75%
15.01	75.00	25%	45%
75.01	or more	15%	40%

Guarantee: Our tapes are guaranteed for ninety days against faulty performance or breakage due to a defect in the tape. For best results, please be sure your tape recorder is in good operating condition and is cleaned regularly.

Mail your order or inquiry to the following address:

Insight for Living
Sales Department
Post Office Box 4444
Fullerton, CA 92634

Quantity discounts and gift certificates are available upon request.

Order Form

Please send me the following cassette tapes:

The current series:　　□ ECS CS Exalting Christ...The Son of God

Individual cassettes:　□ ECS 1　□ ECS 2　□ ECS 3

　　　　　　　　　　　□ ECS 4　□ ECS 5　□ ECS 6

I am enclosing:

$_____　　To purchase the cassette series for $34.50 (in Canada $43.75*) which includes the album cover

$_____　　To purchase individual tapes at $5.00 each (in Canada $6.35*)

$_____　　Total of purchases

$_____　　If the order will be delivered in California, please add 6 percent sales tax

$_____　　U.S. residents please add 10 percent for first-class shipping and handling if desired

$_____　　*British Columbia residents please add 6 percent sales tax

$_____　　Canadian residents please add 7 percent for postage

$_____　　**Overseas residents please add appropriate postage** (See postage chart under "Overseas Ordering Information.")

$_____　　As a gift to the Insight for Living radio ministry for which a tax-deductible receipt will be issued

$_____　　**Total amount due (Please do not send cash.)**

Form of payment:

□ Check or money order made payable to Insight for Living

□ Credit card (Visa or MasterCard only)

If there is a balance:　□ apply it as a donation　□ please refund

---

Credit card purchases:

□ Visa　　□ MasterCard number _____

Expiration date _____

Signature _____

We cannot process your credit card purchase without your signature.

Name _____

Address _____

_____

City _____

State/Province _____ Zip/Postal code _____

Country _____

Telephone (_____) _____ Radio station ___ ___ ___ ___

Should questions arise concerning your order, we may need to contact you.